MECHANICS··
MERCANTILE
LIBRARY.

A Higher Form of Cannibalism?

A HIGHER
FORM OF
CANNIBALISM?

*Adventures in the
Art and Politics of Biography*

Carl Rollyson

Ivan R. Dee
CHICAGO 2005

www.ivanrdee.com

Library of Congress Cataloging-in-Publication Data:
Rollyson, Carl E. (Carl Edmund)
  A higher form of cannibalism? : adventures in the art and politics of biography / Carl Rollyson.
        p. cm.
Includes bibliographical references and index.
ISBN 1-56663-642-6 (alk. paper)
  1. Biography as a literary form. I. Title.
CT21.R59 2005
920'.009—dc22
                    2004061852

In Memory of Ted and Carole Klein

Acknowledgments

I WISH TO THANK, first of all, the members of the Biography Seminar at New York University for years of stimulating discussions that helped to shape the character of this book. I am especially indebted to seminar leaders Brenda Wineapple, Kenneth Silverman, and the late Frederick Karl. Not only did they give me the opportunity to present my work in progress, but they also brought to the seminar guest speakers who provoked me to refine my thoughts about the genre.

Frederick Karl deserves special mention here for his editing of *Biography and Source Studies*, which became another outlet for me to explore my reflections on the troubling aspects of biographical research. He encouraged me to write at great length and with unsparing candor about my failures and successes. I do not believe there was another venue of publication that could have been as hospitable or understanding. AMS Press deserves commendation for publishing a hardcover annual that has no rival when it comes to revealing the biographer at work.

I must also single out my partners in crime: the late Carole Klein, Ann Waldron, and Marion Meade, who shared with me their experience of doing unauthorized biographies. For a time we formed a kind of subgroup of the Biography Seminar, commiserating with one another and offering encouraging advice.

My birth as a biographer really begins with a publication in *Biography*. In 1978, the first year of that journal's publication, my article on Norman Mailer's biography of Marilyn Monroe appeared. The first sentence of that piece owes its life to the journal's editor, George Simson, who cut my verbose opening and began with an abrupt statement that now seems prophetic: "An uneasiness exists in the rationalizations biographers provide for their profession." George's successor, Craig Howes, has not only contributed valuable material for this book but has granted me permission to reproduce my discussions of Johnson, Boswell, and Kitty Kelley that first appeared in *Biography*.

I also thank Panthea Reid Broughton for sending me her file of reviews and commentary on her biography of Virginia Woolf. Jeffrey Meyers has been an indefatigable source of knowledge and support. Paul John Eakin responded to my queries and helped shape my thinking about the biographer's ethics. And no one has contributed more to the shaping of this book than Doug Munro, whose e-mails and steady stream of snail mailings has kept me abreast of what I choose to call a bloodsport. Only one other person has a greater claim on my gratitude, and that is my wife, Dr. Lisa Paddock, without whose editorial eye and legal acumen I would be lost.

It takes time and monetary support to write books. I have been very fortunate to receive a National Endowment for the Humanities fellowship that made it possible for me to do the essential research and thinking during my sabbatical year. Similarly, the dean's office of Baruch College, The City University of New York, and my colleagues on the research and travel committee spurred the completion of this book by releasing me from some teaching responsibilities. Finally, I am very grateful to my colleagues in the Research Award Program of PSC-CUNY for providing the funding to do my archival work at the University of Tulsa. There I found Lori Curtis, head of Special Collections at McFarlin Library, an eager and helpful resource. I have never consulted a more organized, efficient, or cheerful special collections department in my twenty-five years of work as a biographer.

C. R.

Cape May County, New Jersey
January 2005

A Higher Form of Cannibalism?

IN THE EARLY 1970s, Rebecca West, a regular reviewer of biographies for the London *Sunday Telegraph*, deplored the modern taste for cutting up lives and rendering the bloody data of biography that made subjects sound pathological. West's outrage occurred some two decades before Joyce Carol Oates coined the term "pathography" in the *New York Times Book Review* in order to express her disgust with a biography of the writer Jean Stafford because the book emphasized Stafford's physical and mental debilitation. Ted Hughes, writing to the biographer Anne Stevenson, decried the prospect of

allowing myself to be dragged out into the bull-ring and teased and pricked and goaded into vomiting up every detail of my life with Sylvia for the higher entertainment of the hundred thousand Eng Lit Profs and graduates who—as you know—feel very little in this case beyond curiosity of quite a low order, the ordinary village kind, popular bloodsport kind, no matter how they robe their attentions in Lit Crit Theology and ethical sanctity.

In an article titled "Biography Becomes a Bloodsport," the *New York Times* book critic Michiko Kakutani began by quoting Oscar Wilde: "Formerly we used to canonize our heroes. . . . The modern method is to vulgarise them. Cheap editions of great books may be delightful, but cheap editions of great men are absolutely detestable." Since Wilde's condemnation of modern biography, it has accelerated its descent into bad taste, according to Kakutani. In her bill of indictment she included Joe McGinnis's *The Last Brother*, an account of Edward Kennedy which blurred the distinction between biographical speculation and fiction; Jeffrey Meyers's *Scott Fitzgerald*, a "voyeuristic" portrait that fastened on the writer's sex life and the size of his penis; Francine du Plessix Gray's *Rage and Fire*, which reduced Flaubert to a "selfish male chauvinist pig."

Kakutani condemned "tasteless biographies" that "mirror the cultural zeitgeist." What had once seemed liberating in Lytton Strachey's debunking of pious Victorian biography had rapidly devolved from refreshing candor to ugly "fact-and-gossip-stuffed hatchet jobs." Even "prize-winning" biographies from university presses dished the dirt. Why? It was due to a culture of celebrity, Kakutani argued, in which the artist's personality usurped the biographer's narrative. And biography paid well, she added, anticipating an *Irish Times* reviewer's observation that "I have no doubt that literary biography, a relatively weak and recent form, has been recruited in recent years to cutting-edge commercialism."

"Dishy" is the word a reviewer used on the front page of the *New York Times Book Review* to describe my biography *Lillian Hellman: Her Legend and Her Legacy*. A newcomer to the warfare over modern biography, I did not realize then what the word meant. I had to ask my agent. The word is a synonym for gossipy. The reviewer did not consider whether Hellman as a subject might invite such treatment; rather she presumed that the dishiness inhered in the biography itself—in the mind of the biographer, in other words.

Similarly, a few reviewers chastised me for emphasizing Hellman's ugliness, even suggesting that because I had written *Marilyn Monroe: A Life of the Actress* I was predisposed to admiring only that kind of beauty. That I was merely reporting physical descriptions of Hellman conveyed to me by her friends and lovers did not matter. The mere fact of reporting, or rather what I chose to emphasize, became my trademark as a biographer. Dwelling on Hellman's appearance, even when it was a striking feature of how people reacted to her, seemed mean-spirited—as if I had deliberately disfigured my subject.

Kakutani attributed the new invasiveness of biography to changing notions of what is public and private. The Anita Hill–Clarence Thomas and Paula Jones–Bill Clinton controversies had stimulated the public's salacious interests. "Salacious," by the way, is the word British reviewers prefer, including those who attacked my portrayal of the Hemingway/Gellhorn marriage in my biography *Beautiful Exile: The Life of Martha Gellhorn* (a revision of *Nothing Ever Happens to the Brave: The Story of Martha Gellhorn*) because I quoted some of Hemingway's more vicious descriptions of her sexual inadequacy. As the critic Hywell Williams put it, biography is "a peepshow on the past—not the real thing."

Kakutani ended her shotgun survey of contemporary biography by stepping back to the century before Wilde and quoting the British writer John Arbuthnot's observation that biography is "one of the new terrors of death." But if she could find this sentiment expressed more than two hundred years ago, what exactly was new about modern bloodsport biography? Well, that question shall be answered in due course.

The London *Observer*'s literary editor Robert McCrum renewed the Kakutani offensive by taking the novelist/biographer Edmund White's remark for a column title: "Biography is the form by which little people take revenge on big people." McCrum invoked James Joyce's aversion to the "biografiend."

Biographers empty or steal lives of their meaning, Janet Malcolm contends in *The Silent Woman*, her influential evisceration of biography. Like many critics of contemporary biography, Malcolm sides with the subjects (victims) and with their families, who must withstand the prying of biographers. She investigates Sylvia Plath's life in order to understand why it has occasioned so many biographies that tend to idealize her and demonize her husband, Ted Hughes, a brilliant English poet and a ruggedly handsome man whom Malcolm believes biographers have maligned.

Malcolm calls biographers professional burglars, voyeurs, and busybodies, rifling through the most intimate parts of their subjects' lives. An elaborate apparatus of notes and other documentation makes biography appear to be a legitimate enterprise, but the scholarly machinery merely masks a crude delving into gossip, she suggests. Malcolm attributes the great popularity of biography to collusion between biographers and readers, both slavering to discover the secrets of other people's lives.

Biographies raise the same sort of ethical concerns Malcolm has identified in her book on journalism, *The Journalist and the Murderer* (1990). The biographer, like the journalist, is driven by reportorial desire, the urge to get a story no matter how it may affect its subjects, their friends, and their families. Like the journalist, the biographer uses the interview to con people into spilling the beans—as she puts it.

Much of *The Silent Woman* concerns the efforts of Ted and Olwyn Hughes to keep the lid on Sylvia Plath's life, to discourage and even censor unlicensed biographical interpretation. Malcolm sympathizes with them, feeling they have a right to protect their privacy, especially when biographers violate it looking to make a buck, or to get an academic promotion, or to punish Ted Hughes for his vile treatment of Sylvia. For Hughes has become the villain of the story. Tales of his violence and womanizing darken the Plath biographical myth. His own poetry is violent, and it is easy to see him as a modern-day Heathcliff. He even hails from Yorkshire, Brontë country, the world of Emily Brontë's *Wuthering Heights.*

Although Ted Hughes had opposed the Plath biographers because he said he wanted to protect the privacy of himself and his family, several biographers have suggested he was merely trying to stifle and even destroy the evidence, which puts him in a bad light. Hughes contributed to this image of himself by destroying one of Plath's journals and by claiming another had been lost. His sister Olwyn, even in Malcolm's sympathetic portrayal of her and her position as a literary executor, harried biographers—including her own authorized biographer Anne Stevenson, whose biography many critics lambasted as the Plath estate's put-up job.

How can Malcolm be so sympathetic to Ted and Olwyn Hughes, especially when Malcolm admits their many faults and mistakes in the treatment of Plath biographers? Because Malcolm sees biography as an epistemologically problematic genre. She doubts that the biographer can know the truth about much of anything. If this is so, no wonder biographers appear to her and others as impertinent and sensationalistic. They deal mainly in melodrama, confecting narratives that provide a factitious coherence to lives that are far more ambiguous than biographers recognize.

This willful side of biography is apparent in Steven Millhauser's *Edwin Mullhouse: The Life and Death of an American Writer 1943–1954 by Jeffrey Cartwright*. A send-up of biography, the novel is divided into "The Early Years," "The Middle Years," "The Late Years"—a parody of Leon Edel's titles in his five-volume biography of Henry James. Jeffrey is Edwin's Boswell, not only faithfully recording the minutiae of the writer's life but also creating situations in which he can observe his subject's life and eventually his death. Millhauser captures both the comic and sinister side of the biographer's devotion to the creative self and the sense in which the subject is the biographer's creation, an extension of his desire to impose a certain order on sometimes trivial, sometimes hazy evidence. The very neatness of Jeffrey's mind calls into question his interpretations and the biographer's obsession to invent a unified self.

I once sat next to Steven Millhauser during an event at the National Arts Club and tried to engage him in a discussion of his novel, but he was having none of it. Clearly I was the enemy. I think I know why. Biographers, in his view, are bogus because they are writing fiction in the guise of nonfiction.

For Malcolm, the biographer is also a suspect—a "perp," as the police say. She raises all sorts of problems with the so-called data biographers collect. Interviews, for example, are done after the subject's death, or, at the very least, after the events that the biographer seeks to study. Memories fade and contradict each other. Witnesses to the events have their own agendas. There is no infallible way to tell the truth. Similarly, letters are unreliable. They seem to fix experience, but they are only expressions of the moment and cannot be taken for the subject's final or complete attitudes.

Malcolm's main target is Paul Alexander, who reconstructs scenes from Plath's life with an immediacy and detail that, she asserts, cannot be verified. Even if some of his details can be traced to letters, interviews, journals, and memoirs, those details are the product of individuals with their own biases. Alexander misleads readers, Malcolm argues, by presenting a story as if it could be objectively told, when the whole mass of it is in fact a collection of subjective accounts.

Perhaps Malcolm read Jean-Paul Sartre's novel *Nausea*. In his diary, Antoine Roquetin, the biographer of Marquis de Rollebon, grapples not only with the meaning of his subject's life but with existence itself, concluding that he cannot finish his biography and cannot justify the meaning of another human being's existence any more than his own. The novel provides keen insights into the biographer's ambivalence about his subject and his sources, and into the way the biographer's life impinges on his subject, sometimes making the biographer feel he is writing a novel of another's life in compensation for the career he himself cannot pursue.

THE BIOGRAPHER JAMES ATLAS has quoted novelist Martin Amis's derision of biography as a "lowly trade." Amis is echoing his nineteenth-century literary forebears. In *Robert Browning: The Private Life*, Iain Finlayson quotes his subject as believing that biographers should "bugger off and take the tools of their filthy business with them." In *The Paper Men* the novelist William Golding updates Browning by portraying the biographer as literally digging in his subject's garbage. Caught by the subject rooting around in the subject's kitchen like a feral animal—or worse, a scavenger feeding off his subject's waste products—the biographer appears as a shit.

In effect, Atlas argues, biographers are accused of wanting to know too much, and knowing too much deprives the subject of dignity. The more that is known about a subject, the less appealing that subject tends to become. "The less you know about a man's life the better," argued Alfred Tennyson. "I thank God day and night that we know nothing about Shakespeare."

The "too much," however, is not so much revelations of private life per se but rather an obsession with sex, Atlas contends: "our insistence on hearing about it and our embarrassment about our insistence on hearing about it. It's our very willingness to peer behind the bedroom door that's prompting all the anxiety." Actually, it is not the readers who peer but the biographer. Readers leer and revel in gossip about sex.

Flaubert's Parrot, Julian Barnes's fictional meditation on Flaubert's life and work, dramatizes Atlas's argument. The narrator, Geoffrey Brathwaite, is not a biographer, but his pursuit of Flaubert is biographical: "Why does the writing make us chase the writer?" he asks. Viewing biography through the metaphor of a trawling net, Brathwaite combs through the major and minor details of Flaubert's life and career, seeking the most intimate contact with his subject and suggesting that "all biographers secretly want to annex and channel the sex-lives of their subjects; you must make your judgment on me as well as on Flaubert."

Atlas does not put a date on when boudoir biography began. In "Digging in The Wild Garden," Margaret Drabble does. The twentieth century, she contends, "has been a history of the onward march of revelation and self-disclosure. We now speak about ourselves and think about ourselves in a way that would have been unthinkable even to the liberated and deliberately shocking members of the Bloomsbury Group."

But actually it is not the whole of the twentieth century that has been marching toward revelation and self-disclosure, she later suggests in the same essay. And it was not biographers who were responsible for sexing up biography but writers—the subjects of literary biography—who brought the biographers to their bedsides. Writers marketed themselves in a way unthinkable to earlier generations of the literary community who never appeared on public platforms, submitted to interviews, or appeared on talk shows. T. S. Eliot, Somerset

Maugham, Elizabeth Bowen, Samuel Beckett, Graham Greene, and James Joyce shied away from self-promotion. An E. M. Forster kept his private life "very private indeed," she adds. Poets did not give public readings as requirements of a book tour. There were no book tours. Drabble regards flamboyant writers like Edith Sitwell and Dylan Thomas as the exception that proves the rule.

Drabble has something of a case—though think of Charles Dickens, Oscar Wilde, and H. G. Wells as performing selves, not to mention Mark Twain, Stephen Crane, and Ernest Hemingway. I wonder if in fact writers in the modern period have as a rule been so self-effacing. Writers in the 1920s were superstars. Rebecca West was able to attract national press and lucrative lecture tours in this period. It seems to me that every generation of writers complains that suddenly it has lost its privacy.

Nevertheless, Drabble persists in believing that in the 1960s the world changed for writers and that "Angus Wilson himself was a herald of that change and he believed in it." Drabble is Wilson's biographer as well as Arnold Bennett's, and she seeks to honor Wilson's special place in changing the way writers and their biographies began to be presented in the 1960s. In 1963 he published *The Wild Garden*, an unusually candid autobiographical work, which was "greeted with a degree of indignation that was very much of its time. In writing of himself and analysing the symbolic structures and psychological material of his own work, Wilson was seen by the old guard as having betrayed trade secrets, having broken some unwritten literary code."

At the same time a volume of *Paris Review* interviews with writers was published. For those not in the know, it is important to point out that the writers always vet these interviews—

in effect rewriting the questions and answers as a dialogue form of autobiography. These performances are usually studied exercises in self-concealment. Drabble notes that "Henry Green the novelist was praised for his *Paris Review* interview by Rebecca West for his stoical modesty whereas Wilson was castigated for writing largely and reverently about his own novels."

Drabble has an interesting explanation of why Wilson broke ranks, so to speak, why he did not observe the niceties: he was not brought up as a member of the club—never indoctrinated in what is the proper thing. At university he studied history, not literature, which meant that he never absorbed the critical theory of high modernism (Eliot's idea of impersonality, for example, or D. H. Lawrence's injunction to trust the tale, not the teller). To Wilson, it seemed natural to investigate authors of texts, who "might or might not wish to mislead their readers about the sources of their material, a fact that any novelist knows." Wilson revealed the sources of his stories: "His own impulse was to spill the beans and to let the skeletons tumble out of the cupboard and to dig up his own corpses, his carefully buried corpses."

Fellow writers such as Cyril Connolly, Stephen Spender, and E. M. Forster were alarmed. If Wilson could do this to himself, he was legitimizing the biographer's prying enterprise. They might be next. Drabble quotes Wilson's 1959 lecture in Lausanne to show that he knew what he was about:

> I would like to end this lecture with a plea for the unfashionable literary criticism which concerns itself with the biography of the author, the sort of criticism which made Edmund Wilson's *The Wound and the Bow* so important and influential a book. The dangers of such criticism are too well established to

need mention, yet what remains mysterious or incomplete or defective in novels so often arises from the depths of the author's own personal conflicts, conflicts that have themselves driven so painfully to split his personality and to fight a sort of civil war within himself.

Like many inquisitive biographers, Angus Wilson became a kind of pariah. Later I will return to this aspect of the war against biographers, in the chapter on Richard Aldington's biography of T. E. Lawrence.

In 1959, Wilson was just slightly ahead of his time, Drabble suggests. In the 1960s the phenomenon of the literary festival led to portraying the writer as a member of the "chattering classes" and as "publicity fodder." The kickoff for this new literary era was the 1963 Edinburgh Festival, which brought together an amazing collocation of writers from Rebecca West to Norman Mailer to Kingsley Amis to Muriel Spark. Not only did writers of different sensibilities clash, writers stood up and gave confessional speeches; one outed himself as gay.

The 1963 Festival was indeed a kind of watershed event. But not until reading Drabble did I realize how strange the event seemed to writers like Rebecca West, the old guard who thought there were certain proprieties, a code of public conduct for writers. Certainly the conference shattered that. Heretofore such conferences had often centered on political events, such as the Spanish Civil War, or on the celebration of a particular writer or literary movement. After 1963, however, conferences became part of the literary calendar, events in writers' lives, not just fairly rare occasions when writers might congregate.

Of course, not every writer is a conference-goer, but the ubiquity of such gatherings (where writers can pick up, by the way, substantial fees and be fawned over) has surely created the idea of the writer as public figure, a writer whose subject is often himself. Could Philip Roth have turned to novels and non-fiction narratives that constantly raise the question of himself as author and as his own character if not for this cultural shift in the writer's role?

The plethora of literary festivals may have been a new phenomenon in itself, but it was also a way for writers to recapture their public role—one steadily diminishing as mass circulation magazines no longer paid high fees for fiction and newspapers no longer treated traveling writers like Rebecca West as good copy. If writers had lost the lucrative lecture tours that had them addressing women's groups and civic organizations, the festivals enhanced the clout of the literary community and attracted reporters.

James Atlas's vision of readers who crave to be shown more and more intimate details about their beloved writers has scarcely been the work of biographers alone. It has been abetted by the writers themselves and by editors. Atlas's evocation of biography in the bedroom reminds me of my editor at W. W. Norton, who signed my wife and me to write a biography of Susan Sontag. He liked our proposal because it professed to take her work seriously and eschewed a gossipy approach to this controversial figure. Even though the rumor mill about Sontag's activities remained in good running order until her recent death, we reported very little of it in our book. Our circumspection did not, however, prevent our editor from calling us from time to time to relay gossip about her, or deflect certain critics from calling our biography gossipy. What they meant, however, was not gossip really, but rather the fact that we had inquired so insistently into how she had built her career by shrewd literary politicking and image enhancement. Even raising such issues, reviewers seemed to feel, made our book unworthy because it detracted from a focus on her work.

Writers like Susan Sontag are sexy subjects—even if the word "sex" is not to be taken literally but is rather a synonym for "enticing" or "provocative." Did she, by the way, ever have a jacket photo of herself that was not glamorized? The photographs are a tease, and part of her tease is that she will not admit that she is teasing. Having her lounge against a background picture of New York City and a stack of books is the hip version of Ingres's *La Grande Odalisque* (1814).

Since the 1960s there certainly has been a changing standard for the portrayal of sex in biographies—as Fiona McCarthy, writing a biography of the artist and craftsman Eric Gill, discovered and welcomed, even though it cost her the confidence of her subject's literary executor, who had given her *carte blanche*. In the Clark Library at UCLA, she read Gill's diaries describing not only his adulteries but also his incestuous relations with his sisters and daughters as well as sexual experiments he conducted with his friends' dog. A relieved biographer felt the entries bolstered her speculations and clarified many aspects of the artist's life she had found puzzling.

Robert Speaight, an earlier Gill biographer and a Gill family friend, had excluded this shocking material from his book, published in 1966. As McCarthy puts it, Speaight saw it as his duty to suppress embarrassing revelations. "Twenty years later, the conventions of biography were considerably altered, frank discussion of the sex life of one's subject being well on its way to becoming de rigueur for biographers. I did not consider for one moment that Speaight's gentlemanly reticence was possible for me," McCarthy concludes.

She showed her biography to the executor before she published it, and he naturally found they differed on some points, but he raised no objection to publication. Then a month later he wrote her in great distress: "our acquaintance and correspondence must cease." The biographer assumed that his change of attitude resulted from the response of Gill's family, who were hostile to the book. She is probably right, since I had virtually the same experience with Michael Foot, the British Labour politician, when writing a biography of his wife, Jill Craigie. He gave me complete freedom and had only the mildest criticisms of the draft I showed him. But then his nephew Paul and a few of Jill's friends began to hector him about the biography, and, as in the case of McCarthy's relationship with Gill's executor, my relationship with Foot has never been the same.

McCarthy attributes her troubles to a lack of experience: It was her first biography, and she thought only of her responsibility to her subject and to her sense of his "bizarre contradictions." But of course Gill's life was interconnected, "stirring emotions, resurrecting memories," and thus the biography became McCarthy's "baptism of fire."

I'm not sure biographers are or ever can be prepared for the assault on their work. Jill Craigie was my seventh biography, and yet I felt like a babe because in retrospect I should have realized that Foot would renege on his promise to give me a free hand. "It's your book," he said, not really meaning it while thinking he meant it. What he ought to have said is, "It's your book, but it's my wife and family, so prepare for the struggle!" Biographers blind themselves to the ramifications of their work—at least while they are doing it—because they are so wrapped up in telling their stories. That others have an interest in the story, that they feel they own it, in a way, is where the bad blood begins to flow.

OTHERS HAVE ARGUED that it is not sex—or gossip about
sex—that is the problem but rather the way biographers sensationalize all intimate matters, or dwell on the "negative aspects of the lives of their subjects," as one member of an
Internet biography chat group put it. "We inhabit an age of
ravenous prurience and philistine envy," wrote Michael Ratcliffe in *The Observer*. "More people are gawping at Iris Murdoch's senility and sex drive than ever enjoyed reading The
Bell." Biography is intrusive, the biographer a transgressor, ex-
ploring "secret weaknesses," as A. S. Byatt puts it in a recent
book review. Thus John Sutherland echoes Ratcliffe by calling
biography part of an "Age of Blackwash."

The venom against biography contains the idea that art is
pure and biography befouls it. "Art is, to a certain extent, sacred. Surely?" asks one troubled Internet forum participant. If
art is sacred, then what does that mean about our attitude toward authors? "When I was young, reading the books, I
thought authors were Gods," the writer Sherman Alexie confessed. "Perhaps, in all of you, there is still some of that child-

like wonder about authors, that worship." Alexie admitted that knowing about writers' lives did affect his reaction to their work. "Maybe I'm just the book lover's equivalent of a lapsed Catholic."

It is not hard to believe that reviewers attack biographers for defiling their gods. Alexie, now in the inner circle of literary life, spoke of himself as "disillusioned" and even perhaps "forever polluted" because he knew so much about writers' lives. When Philip Hensher finds that parts of Peter Conradi's *Iris Murdoch: A Life* do not help illuminate her work, the reviewer concludes that the biography "inevitably starts to seem prurient. It's not altogether Conradi's fault—and it should be said that this is a good, tactful biography—but rather the fault of the genre."

Biography, in fact, is regarded by some critics not as a genre but as a kind of butcher's business. Thus a reviewer in the British *Independent* refers to the "vast sausage-machine of the biography industry," and an *Observer* commentator calls James King a "practiced academic biographer (William Blake's scalp and Paul Nash's among his trophies)." Biography becomes a kind of greasy product, in some critics' minds, because it offers the "repetitive pleasures" of pornography, concludes a writer in *New Statesman and Society*.

An admirer of my *Lillian Hellman* wrote to me that she had not "picked a victim" yet, but she was giving serious thought to writing a biography. How did one go about it? she wanted to know. The biographer, after all, has enormous power, selecting those aspects of a life to emphasize, those parts to leave out. Like a novel, a biography is a story in which characters are manipulated and moved about to suit a controlling sensibility. My attraction to the form derives from this urge to reconstitute a life within the covers of a book.

I don't blame anyone for feeling victimized by the biogra-fiend. In miniature, a biography is rather like having to sit still for a photograph that you do not want taken of yourself. You're robbed in some way of your substance. And you are probably not consoled by the biografiend's insistence that he or she admires you and must have a picture.

Biography, in some readers' minds, resembles "true crime" books. "She boiled squirrel nutkin, he diddled girls"—begins one *Salon* thread about biography. "Beatrix Potter vivisected, boiled, bisected and dissected," the thread continues. Biogra-phy, then, is regarded as a kind of sadism. In a *Readerville.com* thread on biography, a participant writes:

> There's a bio out there of Lewis Carroll that I was really de-pressed to read about—focuses on his attraction to little girls and how he tried hard to overcome his "unnatural urges." The poor God-fearing and idealistic writer. He was certainly no pe-dophile, and he wrote such amazing books. So, he may have sublimated some urges. But, do we really need to go into the detail of that? How is that going to make me appreciate his writing better? Shouldn't this approach be rightfully denigrated as pathography?

Paul John Eakin, who includes a section entitled "Bloodsport Biography" in *The Ethics of Life Writing*, concludes that "all parties to the biographical enterprise seem to concede that bi-ography has the potential to assault—symbolically—the very person of its subject." Reviewing the Gelbs' biography of Eu-gene O'Neill, Joseph J. Ellis, a renowned biographer of Thomas Jefferson, John Adams, and others, asserts:

> A good deal of modern biography, especially when the subject is a major literary figure, is driven by the urge to undermine the

writer's artistic achievement by exposing the previously un-known details of his or her private life. Or as John Updike re-cently put it, literary biographies seem designed "to reduce celebrities to a set of antics and ailments to which we can feel superior." O'Neill's early life would seem to provide a veritable arsenal of ammunition for this emerging genre, which we might call "homicidal biography."

"There are those who argue," writes the biographer Nicholas Shakespeare, "that biography is itself a kind of murder."

A crime may not actually be committed, but readers think of biography as a bloody conflict between biographer and sub-ject. "Sometimes one senses a struggle going on, between the lines—one man trying to conceal, one to reveal; two people wrestling over one's self-definition," writes a biography chat-group participant. This struggle is apparent at the end of *The Real Life of Sebastian Knight*, in which Vladimir Nabokov's narrator/biographer, who is also his subject's half brother, concludes the novel with an equivocation: "I am Sebastian, or Sebastian is I, or perhaps we both are someone whom neither of us knows." Part of the hostility toward biography and biog-raphers has to do with the reader/critic's belief that no one can speak for another, and that those who try to do so are violat-ing a precious boundary between oneself and another.

Nabokov's novel speaks to the strange and sometimes tor-tured intimacy the biographer shares with his subject, an inti-macy that can result in loathing. "The longer a biographer works on a subject, the more his hostility seems to increase, until he begins to hate the subject for devouring his own life," writes Jeffrey Meyers, a professional biographer. Only in one instance can I affirm Meyers's observation. Martha Gellhorn called my biography of her a "paean of hate." Actually, I never did come to dislike her, even though she did try various means to prevent publication of my biography. Susan Sontag is another story.

Living subjects of biographies have thought of their struggle with biographers as a life-and-death matter. Not only did Gellhorn employ a legal firm to threaten my publisher with a libel action, she tried to enlist the Author's Guild on her behalf—mistakenly believing that biographers, unlike herself, did not deserve the respect of this organization. The Guild replied to her: "How can we take one writer's side against another's?"

After Gellhorn's death in 1998, I decided to revise my biography of her, which had been published in the United States but not in Great Britain. Gellhorn had easily blocked the book's appearance in countries where the libel law places the burden on the author and publisher to prove their innocence. In the United States a libel action requires the plaintiff to prove her case, and subjects of biographies rarely win such cases—though if they have sufficient funds they may file lawsuits as a punitive measure, hoping the publisher will cancel the book rather than incur significant legal costs. My American publisher, St. Martin's Press, stuck by me and employed a law firm to vet my book.

Even the threat of a libel action in Britain is often enough to scare off publishers. Gellhorn's literary executor, Sandy Matthews (her stepson), hearing that I would publish this time in Britain, renewed the vendetta, sending me a threatening letter and warning me that I would not be permitted to quote from her work.

Matthews's letter was just the opening shot. Even before my book appeared, the *Times* of London ran an article by Georgina Howell summarizing my book. I had no control over this piece, arranged through my publisher. But John Pilger, one of Gellhorn's friends gunning for me, immediately sent off a complaining letter (before my book's publication date), which the *Times* printed.

I rarely reply to such attacks, believing that my biographies are fair game. But in this case I determined early on that not to engage my critics would leave my book bloodied beyond repair. A well-orchestrated campaign can kill a book, and such campaigns are more easily engineered in London, where the literary world is much closer knit and even more incestuous than the prevailing coteries in New York City.

Since author's replies are almost always a losing game—they merely appear to be self-serving and regarded as expressions of hurt feelings—I simply corrected factual errors in the letters and articles about my book. There were not many negative reviews, as it turned out, but even the handful of hostile critics did not hear a word from me.

Here is what I wrote in response to Pilger:

> In his attack on my book, *Beautiful Exile: The Life of Martha Gellhorn*, John Pilger writes: "In the Howell piece, his assertions and those of the *Sunday Times* are impossible to distinguish." What a curious thing to say and to rush into print with such an inept commentary. If Mr. Pilger would read my book, he would have no trouble making a distinction. His quarrel is with Howell, not with me.

"The Woman's Hour," a BBC radio program, then set up an ambush. When I arrived at the studio, I learned that Pilger (by phone) and a Gellhorn friend (a fellow female journalist whose name I have forgotten) would be there to "discuss" Gellhorn's life. Not a bit of it, as the British say. They were there to traduce me.

Pilger began by accusing me of cowardice, publishing my book after Gellhorn had died. But that was ridiculous, since I had first published in 1990 and Gellhorn had spent nearly a decade afterward attacking me. He also attempted to suggest that my book was so scandalous that it could not be published in Britain until Gellhorn's death. By this time the book had been published, but it was obvious that neither Pilger nor his ally had read it, since they claimed, for example, that I had no documentation for my book. Then Pilger misstepped, launching into a paean to Gellhorn's feminism—an absurd mischaracterization of her that even his female ally could not brook. Consequently the two of them got into a squabble. As I pointed out to the BBC interviewer, "You see the difficulty of writing biographies when two of Gellhorn's friends cannot agree about certain basic facts."

But Pilger & Co. would not let up. Next I replied to a letter to the *Sunday Times* that attacked the authenticity of my book, especially my description of a love affair between Gellhorn and H. G. Wells, and of Gellhorn's rather insensitive treatment of her son:

> I doubted whether I should respond to the letter of April 15, 2001, attacking my biography of Martha Gellhorn since the letter writers have not read it, but perhaps it will serve your readers to point out the following: 1. H. G. Wells describes in detail his love affair with Martha Gellhorn in a long suppressed memoir. 2. Nowhere in my book do I suggest Gellhorn was afflicted with self-hatred. 3. What I say in the book about Gellhorn's attitude toward her adopted son Sandy Gellhorn is a mild paraphrase of the much harsher verdict explicitly stated in her letters. 4. While I did not have access to all of Gellhorn's papers, many of her letters were available in archives—all of which are cited in my biography.

Sandy Gellhorn, Gellhorn's adopted son, never publicly attacked my book. And I thought it rather revealing that Gellhorn had handed over the job of roughing me up to Sandy Matthews, who certainly carried on her lust for battle.

Matthews's next ploy was to get a *Telegraph* reporter (dupe would be a better term) to interview him about my book. By this point, surely, he could at least have read it. Instead he was clearly responding to reviews, which had confused him with Sandy Gellhorn. Since Sandy Matthews had written me a threatening letter, and since the narrative in both editions of my book is clear on the difference between the two Sandys, I can only conclude that Matthews deliberately misled the *Telegraph* reporter who did not bother to check with me when she said I had "muddled up" the two Sandys. I wrote a two-sentence letter of clarification, which the *Telegraph* printed.

It must seem that I have gone into too much self-serving detail about just one book, but here, in the sequel, is why it matters for students of bloodsport biography. When Trafalgar Square Press distributed the UK edition of my revised Gellhorn biography in the United States, *Publishers Weekly* repeated the disinformation campaign waged in the British press. *PW*'s negative review, I later learned directly from one of its editors, had drawn directly on false statements made by British reporters about my book. The *PW* reviewer, apparently hostile to the very idea of my biography, had not bothered to look for any of my letters in the British press, especially this one to the *Guardian*:

> The headline reads "Audrey Gillian investigates." Apparently that investigation did not include attempting to contact me, the author of Beautiful Exile: The Life of Martha Gellhorn. Gillian reports that Gellhorn wrote 2 5 pages of notes

about my errors. I wrote to Victoria Glendinning, one of Martha's friends who reviewed my biography of Rebecca West quite favorably, and asked her to point out my mistakes. She replied that she did not believe there were mistakes but rather that Gellhorn was simply opposed to my doing the book. Gellhorn contributed to my biography of Lillian Hellman and certainly did not respond to me as a biographer peddling salacious material. Indeed, she sent a letter complimenting me on one of my articles and only became hostile when she found herself the subject of my work. Gellhorn's "friends" have had ten years, by the way, to seriously refute the first edition of my book and they have not done so. Nor did Gellhorn force any changes in the first edition of the book. She only threatened a legal case. I don't believe, in fact, that these "friends" of Gellhorn's have even read my book. Certainly they have not read Francis King's review in *The Literary Review*. He calls my biography "perceptive, well researched and well written."

After a firm letter from me, *PW* ran a retraction on June 10, 2002:

> Correction: In our review of Carl Rollyson's *Beautiful Exile: The Life of Martha Gellhorn* (Forecasts, Apr. 8), we stated that "Gellhorn's successful lawsuit . . . forced (Rollyson) to retract portions of his first biography of her (*Nothing Ever Happens to the Brave*), published in 1990." In fact, there was no such lawsuit, nor did Rollyson retract any portion of the biography. PW regrets the error and apologizes to Mr. Rollyson.

The damage, of course, had been done. Stating there was a successful lawsuit sounds like a fact, not an opinion, which is what makes such malicious reviews especially destructive. A few years later, at a symposium on biography in Manhattan, an audience member asked me why I had had to retract certain portions of my Gellhorn biography. Retractions never really retract.

Roger Straus, Susan Sontag's publisher, actually commanded a Norton editor, who also published books with Straus's firm (Farrar, Straus & Giroux), to "kill the fucker [he regarded the Sontag biography as a profanity]." When the editor did not obey, FSG dropped his own novel from its list.

Even more notorious instances of the battle between biographers and their subjects—such as J. D. Salinger's campaign against Ian Hamilton—will be canvased in later chapters of this book. Suffice it to say here that Salinger's withdrawal from public life and from publication reflects a horror of a prying readership, signaled in his story *Seymour: An Introduction*, in which the narrator remarks that "our gusto for the lurid or the partly lurid (which, of course, includes both low and superior gossip) is probably the last of our fleshy appetites to be sated or effectively curbed. A good many people respond with a special impetus, a zing, even, in some cases, to artists and poets who as well as having a reputation for producing great or fine art have something garishly Wrong with them as persons; a spectacular flaw. . . . God have mercy on the lonely bastards."

Paul Bowles's reaction to his unauthorized biographer, Christopher Sawyer-Lauçanno, was to send him a letter of "recrimination and accusation"—to quote Bowles's own words. "I regret not having arranged for [the biographer's] poisoning on his first visit to Tangier," Bowles wrote in another letter.

Such vituperation is not uncommon. Doris Lessing, John le Carré, John Cheever, Bernard Malmud, Saul Bellow, Eudora Welty, Woody Allen, Stephen Spender, and the estates of many other writers have made it difficult—sometimes impossible—for biographers to proceed. When Jeffrey Meyers approached le Carré about a biography, the subject promised neither to help nor to hinder the biographer. But when Meyers proceeded with his usual zest, le Carré reneged and began telling friends to snub Meyers, who dropped his project after fighting a rearguard action against le Carré's attacks (through his lawyers, agents, and publicists).

Some writers (Norman Mailer, William Styron, and Joyce Carol Oates, for example) try to defang biographers by carefully controlling access to their archives and by handpicking their Boswells. Sometimes the ploy backfires—as in the case of Gore Vidal's futile attempt to restrain Fred Kaplan, who forced Vidal to stick by their original agreement not to interfere. In effect the biographer (domesticated or wild) is regarded with extreme wariness, if not rage.

WHAT ARE THE ORIGINS of this contemporary denunciation of biography as bloodsport? Individual biographies have always been subject to attack, but since when has the genre itself been rejected as somehow underhanded and even as a kind of mugging? Biography has "long had a bad history," Margaret Drabble remarks. In surveying the "first golden age of British biography" epitomized by Johnson and Boswell, she notes that their shady Grub Street contemporaries were mocked by John Dryden for Judas-like treachery. Similarly, Joseph Addison decried this degraded "race of men," which engaged in death-watches for the purpose of making a penny out of their biographical subjects.

When Oscar Wilde remarked, "Formerly we used to canonize our heroes . . . ," how far back did he mean to go? Did he have in mind the Victorian practice of excising from biographies events or character traits that reduced the subject's stature? Then it was enough to write an idealized, bowdlerized, life-and-letters treatment of a subject that a Victorian public accepted, indeed craved, in a century that celebrated progress and prosperity. Without an aggressive market mentality, like that manifested by twentieth-century publishers, biography as a genre, with a few significant exceptions, languished in the nineteenth century. It was a reliable but staid form of literature. Elizabeth Gaskell, for example, withheld from her biography what she knew about Charlotte Brontë's infatuation with her Belgian tutor, a married man, to whom she wrote passionate letters. Mrs. Gaskell sought successfully to shift attention away from her subject's bold literary work— Jane Eyre did not seem to behave like a proper Victorian woman—and portray Charlotte as the dutiful, self-sacrificing, and virtually sainted sister who bore her brother's profligacy with Christian patience while obeying her father's wishes and preserving and nurturing her siblings' work and the world's interest in them. In her lifetime, Charlotte Brontë's novels had been called "coarse"; Mrs. Gaskell's biography aimed to rehabilitate Charlotte as a lady who also happened to write.

In other words, Mrs. Gaskell, who felt the pressures of conventional womanhood—her biographer Jenny Uglow shows that it was sometimes a strain to maintain a home and career—minimized the problem in her biography of Charlotte Brontë, making her biographical subject more like the biographer than the evidence of Brontë's life warrants.

It was, of course, this kind of conventionalization of the subject that Lytton Strachey would ridicule in his sardonic *Eminent Victorians*. Strachey was hailed as a revolutionary, bringing a refreshing candor to a stuffy genre, when in fact he was merely returning biography to its robust, eighteenth-century manner, a golden age of life writing. Wilde himself had his share of fun with the earnest Victorians. Yet when it came to biography—even though he had made his own personality of a piece with his work—he condemned the biographer's quest for intimate details of the kind that James Anthony Froude depicted in his life of Thomas Carlyle, a much vilified work because of its revelations about Carlyle's private life, especially his marriage. Even the careful Mrs. Gaskell was thought to have published too much of Charlotte's private correspondence. For a nineteenth-century biography, it is remarkably revealing. She included intimate anecdotes in order to create an absorbing story that made the Brontës' lives as compelling as fiction. The gap between Mrs. Gaskell and Paul Alexander, in other words, is not as wide as certain critics would suppose.

In the United States, until very recently, biographers have been reticent about their subjects' faults and failings. Although Boswell's candor was widely praised in American periodicals, virtually no biographer attempted anything like his comprehensive approach to biography. As Scott E. Caspar documents in *Constructing American Lives*, nineteenth-century American biographers, committed to nation building and inspiring stories, eschewed discussion of their subjects' private lives. Plenty of scandalous material was available. The press certainly carried reports of Thomas Jefferson's slave mistress Sally Hemings, and Alexander Hamilton made a sensational public confession of his extramarital affair, which led to his lover's husband's blackmailing Hamilton. Biographers, however, until well into the twentieth century, did not take seriously the Sally Hemings story. Indeed, when Fawn Brodie published *Thomas Jefferson: An Intimate Biography* in 1974, her fellow historians excoriated her for lending weight to so much gossip. When Annette Gordon-Reed, a New York law school professor—it is significant that she was not a professional biographer—suggested in *Thomas Jefferson and Sally Hemings: An American Controversy* that he might well have had a sexual relationship with Hemings, distinguished biographers such as

Joseph J. Ellis roundly rejected her assessment—and then had to recant when the DNA evidence corroborated this maverick biographer's findings.

Wilde's hostility to biography is really aimed at literary biography. It is hard for me to believe that he would have cared if Disraeli or Gladstone, for example, had received the blood-sport treatment. And so it is with most diatribes against biography, which presume that literary figures are somehow sacrosanct and that literature—look at the word used for it, the "canon"—is as holy as the books of the Bible. The biographer in effect produces apocrypha—everything that is not supposed to be part of the official story—unless the biography is "authorized" or blessed. All others are unauthorized or damned.

These distinctions, however, will not hold, as Henry James, the founding father of biophobia, foretold at the turn of the twentieth century. Sooner or later, whether the biographer is authorized or not, he joins the criminal classes. In James's *The Aspern Papers*, an erstwhile biographer of Jeffrey Aspern, an early nineteenth-century poet, visits Venice hoping to acquire the correspondence between Aspern and his mistress, Miss Bordereau. Insinuating himself into Miss Bordereau's life, the biographer takes her niece, Tita, into his confidence. After Miss Bordereau catches him searching through her desk, he leaves for a few days. When he returns after a fortnight, he finds that she has died. Tita has fallen in love with him and intimates that only a relative can be permitted to examine the papers. Alarmed at this proposal, the biographer leaves, only to find at his next meeting with Tita that she has destroyed the letters. This is the story in which James coins a memorable term for the biographer: a "publishing scoundrel."

It is significant that the biographer himself tells the tale. He suffers from a bad conscience, but he is also trying to rationalize the importance of his task and why he resorted to un-ethical means to secure his documents. The quest for intimate knowledge overcomes his moral scruples. At times he is almost jocular about his violation of social conventions—a mood I understand very well. The very idea of transgression affirms the momentousness of the biography; the subject is so great that it becomes a crime, in the biographer's eyes, to desist from capturing his prize. The biographer's ego, in other words, becomes fused with his desire to render his subject's story.

In "The Real Right Thing," James's other exercise in bio-phobia, George Withermore, an inexperienced young journalist and critic, is flattered by an invitation from the widow of the great writer Ashton Doyne to write her recently deceased husband's biography. She gives him complete access to Doyne's papers and puts him to work in the writer's study. Withermore immerses himself in Doyne's archive and at first is encouraged by the almost palpable presence of his subject. Then he begins to have second thoughts.

James wrote this tale while embarking on a biography of the American poet and sculptor William Wetmore Story. As Leon Edel suggests in his biography of James, the novelist seems to have wondered whether he was doing the right thing in abandoning fiction for biography. "The Real Right Thing" reads like a Gothic ghost story, with the biographer portrayed as a kind of grave robber, awakening the spirit of the deceased. James, of course, did not invent this attitude toward biography, but he blackens the biographical quest as if to shrive himself. In fact, "The Real Right Thing" is cloaked in black. Doyne's widow greets the biographer in her "large array of mourning—with big black eyes, her big black wig, her big black fan and gloves. . . ." She encourages the biographer to work in the evenings "for quiet and privacy." But those evening sessions reveal that the biographer is working in the dark. It is on such a "black London November" that Withermore begins to doubt he has the right to plumb Doyne's life: "What warrant had he ever received from Ashton Doyne himself for so direct and, as it were, so familiar an approach?" Still, for nearly a month the biographer labors to believe in the "consecration of his enterprise."

Words like "warrant" and "consecration" suggest just how badly biographers want to believe they are blessed. This self-delusion is what leads Stephen Oates, for example, to announce in his biography of Faulkner that his subject appeared to him in a dream to sanction Oates's enterprise. I cannot think of anything more unlikely than Faulkner, a writer with a great Gothic imagination and a detestation of prying biographers, spending a moment in his afterlife to anoint Oates. It is far more likely that Oates, like Withermore, misread the meaning of his subject's appearance. In this case, Oates apparently failed to spot the horsewhip in Faulkner's hand.

Biographers are moles, trespassers, and burglars, as James dramatizes by having Withermore "dipping, deep into some of Doyne's secrets." The biographer delights in "drawing curtains, forcing many doors, reading many riddles, going, in general, as they said, behind almost everything." Biographers go for the back story, the hidden side of the subject's face, as Edel himself acknowledged with relish when he changed a Jamesian term, "the figure in the carpet," to describe the biographer's quest to find the "figure under the carpet." That cliché about sweeping things under the carpet becomes a Gothic horror in the biographer's mission. So deluded is Withermore at one point that he imagines Doyne's presence as a kind of breath of the Holy Spirit lingering over the "young priest at his altar." It does not occur to the biographer, so dedicated to resurrecting a life, that to others he is creating a kind of Frankenstein, a semblance of a human being but certainly not "the real right thing." His enterprise is not right morally and not right aesthetically.

It is precisely at the moment of his exaltation that Withermore senses Doyne's withdrawal from him. The biographer's "protected state"—largely a figment of his imagination—disintegrates, and doubts about his business begin to gather. Now the biographer experiences the "monstrous oppression" of his subject, who becomes a burden the biographer cannot tolerate. Suddenly the widow appears as "the tall black lady." Withermore no longer feels in league with her but rather on the other side, so to speak—that is, on the side of his subject, who is signaling through Withermore's uneasiness Doyne's wish that the biography should proceed no further. "I feel I'm wrong," the biographer tells the widow. Rather than giving his subject a new life, Withermore contends that in writing about Doyne, "We lay him bare. We serve him up. What is it called? We give him to the world." Exposing his "original simplicity" as a misunderstanding, the biographer concludes, "But I understand at last. He only wanted to communicate. He strains forward out of his darkness; he reaches toward us out of his mystery; he makes us dim signs out of his horror." The uncomprehending widow replies, "Horror?" Withermore explains: "At what we're doing. . . . He's there to *save* his life. He's there to be let alone." The widow, thinking only of the precious biography, "almost shrieked": "So you give up." Like a character in a Gothic tale, she exclaims: "You *are* afraid!" And indeed, the biographer is terrified, telling her that Doyne is "there as a curse!" And the curse carries moral and spiritual weight: "I *should* give up!" Withermore emphasizes.

The widow has seen the biography as a gift to her husband, a tribute to his importance. The biographer essays one more attempt to climb the stairs to his subject's study, only to return to say that Doyne is on the threshold, "guarding it." So Withermore did not enter? she asks. "He forbids!" Withermore says in such a commanding voice that after an instant the widow concedes, "Give up." She decides to mount the stairs herself but returns, acknowledging that her dead husband still blocks the way. "I give up," are her last words.

By and large, biographers who do not give up do not wish to confront the harrowing aspects of biography. I have heard biographers joke about their work in archives, saying they like to read other people's mail. I think they find it comforting that those documents are housed in a public repository, as if such institutions sanction their research. Even better, if the biographer can wangle a supporting grant, it is another sign of approval. But the truth is that biography remains invasive, however you dress it up.

I am reminded of an incident that occurred while Mrs. Gaskell was researching her life of Charlotte Brontë. Unlike James's biographer in *The Aspern Papers*, Mrs. Gaskell did not try to obtain certain papers by subterfuge. Instead she resorted to intimidation and surprise attack in order to secure the unpublished manuscript of *The Professor* and other items. She had been at work on the Brontë biography for a year and realized she could not complete the work without once more visiting Haworth Parsonage, where Charlotte's father, Patrick, and her husband, the Reverend Arthur Nicholls, stood watch over the Brontë collection.

In *The Brontë Myth*, Lucasta Miller succinctly sums up Mrs. Gaskell's plan of attack: "Too nervous to brave the Parsonage on her own, this time Gaskell chose as her chaperon the overbearing Sir James Kay-Shuttleworth. His remarkable insensitivity to others' feelings meant that he was able to make quite shameless demands without embarrassment." Sir James, moreover, made it possible for Mrs. Gaskell to remain a lady while she reaped the benefits of his rudeness. She could not have been more delighted—as she confessed to Charlotte's publisher George Smith:

> I have had a very successful visit to Haworth . . . accompanied by Sir J P. K Shuttleworth, to whom it is evident that both Mr Brontë & Mr Nicholls look up.—& who is not prevented by the fear of giving pain from asking in a peremptory manner for whatever he thinks desirable. He was extremely kind in forwarding all my objects; and coolly took possession of many things while Mr Nicholls was saying he could not possibly part with them.

Reading this passage in Miller's wonderful account of how biographies have shaped the Brontë myth, I experienced, as a biographer, the shock of recognition. For I had employed almost the same stratagem while researching the life of Susan Sontag, when I asked my wife, Lisa Paddock (like me a University of Toronto–trained Ph.D. in English, and an attorney), to be my co-author. I believed that including her on the team, so to speak, would set up the sort of passive/aggressive approach that Mrs. Gaskell relished. If she, in effect, hid behind a man, I was perfectly willing to conceal myself behind a woman. Like Mrs. Gaskell and Sir James, my wife and I had met our subject (though in our case only once), and we had both been entranced by her presence—as Mrs. Gaskell and Sir James had been by Charlotte.

We approached friends of the well-defended Sontag (she made it clear she wanted no biography) by rehearsing, in an almost gushing fashion, our sole encounter with her while we were teaching in Poland. Even though our meeting with her was brief, she had charmed and inspired us. It was in this spirit that we wrote to William Phillips, editor of *Partisan Review*, which had published her famous essay, "Notes on 'Camp,'" and other pieces that had established her as what Norman Podhoretz called the "dark lady" of American letters. Phillips was proud of championing Sontag, but he did not answer our letter. During our interview with Richard Sennett, Sontag's colleague at New York University's Humanities Institute, he brought up Phillips's importance in making Sontag's reputation, and we voiced our regret that so far we had been unable to speak to Phillips. Sennett, an interviewee who liked to be helpful and perhaps enjoyed the power he had to assist our quest, encouraged us to use his name. We did.

Phillips took our mention of Sennett as a sign that we were Sontag's authorized biographers, although we had neither stated nor implied that such was the case. By the time we arrived at his Lincoln Center apartment, dripping wet from a downpour that presaged rough sailing, he had evidently received a call from Sontag. Now we encountered a recalcitrant figure who could not be budged. In poor health, he occupied his chair like a stone statue or a truculent Buddha—until I hit upon the idea of asking him about his *Partisan Review* memoir. He agreed to comment, but he became increasingly upset as I focused on page references to Sontag.

This is where Lisa became vital. She had almost immediately established a rapport with Phillips's companion, Edith Kurzweil. While I did something like a Sir James act—I kept asking questions even as Phillips crustily replied with terse answers—Lisa smiled . . . and smiled . . . and smiled at Edith, as if sharing some kind of secret knowledge women have about men (no matter what age) who go at it like rambunctious puppies. In the midst of this male tugging back and forth, Edith kept saying, "Talk to them, William." But Phillips had checked with Sontag and was on orders not to talk.

As we were preparing to leave, Kurzweil took a phone call and waved goodbye. I was still concentrating on Phillips, attempting, with some success, to pry answers out of him as I was backing out of his apartment. Lisa studied Kurzweil, still on the phone. Lisa could tell the call was from Sontag and heard Kurzweil running down the list of people we said we had interviewed and some of the questions we had posed to Phillips.

In our notes to *Susan Sontag: The Making of an Icon*, we explained the circumstances of the Phillips interview, and at least one reviewer deplored our taking advantage of a very old man. Most biographers, including Mrs. Gaskell, do not say much about how they obtain their interviews, in part because they do not wish to offend their sources, and in part because they do not wish to divulge the obnoxious tricks of the trade.

You might almost think there is a Special Secrets Act for biographers. An exception is the redoubtable Jeffrey Meyers, who includes an essay in *The Spirit of Biography* about how he hounded the formidable Martha Gellhorn into an interview about Hemingway. When he had no success via the mails, he simply showed up at her London flat and slipped a note under her door. She answered by opening the door and telling him she would get a stomachache if she had to discuss her ex-husband. And yet she relented and allowed the relentless Meyers to question her. As a result he was the only biographer to have a really solid face-to-face interview with her.

Inspired by Meyers's brashness, I decided to show up unannounced at Gellhorn's Welsh cottage, which she had named Catscradle. The day (August 8, 1989) was getting on toward sunset, the sky turning into darker hues of blue merging into vivid pockets of light, the green countryside subsiding into shadows. I was beginning to doubt that I would be able to take the photograph of Catscradle that I wanted for my biography. I had never been to Wales and had only the vaguest address to go by. Ron and Beryl Gadd, who have lived in Wales all of their lives, were driving my wife and me through Chepstow, a name that Gellhorn had put on an address label I had found in her mother's papers. Ron pulled over to the side of the road, and Beryl began asking people if they had heard of Catscradle, which was supposed to be in New Church West. No one recognized it, but Beryl persisted—on one occasion getting out of the car to ask for directions at a home with a fiercely barking dog. I watched her from the comfort of my back seat, deciding not to test the dog's intentions (not the last time I would hide behind a woman). After some confused consultation of a map at the Gwent Constabulary and a discussion with a friendly constable, we set off on the road to Shirenewton, which we were assured would take us to New Church West. On the way—certain that we had gone too far—we stopped at a pub. This time (thinking it was safe) I got out, curious to see the interior. No one had heard of Catscradle, but we were on the road to New Church West all right, and they did have places with names like Catscradle—"the Rampant Cat and such." Another stop: we approached a home with what sounded like a very large dog barking loudly behind a door. I stood behind Beryl as she knocked. After several seconds a friendly woman appeared, and I finally found my tongue, "Does Martha Gellhorn live around here?" Her reply startled me, for I had not expected her first words to so exactly recall the way people react when they recognize the name: "The wife of the famous writer?"

Now it seemed just possible that I would come face-to-face with Martha Gellhorn. I had written her after I had started work on my biography, sent her my biography of Marilyn Monroe and a piece on William and Estelle Faulkner, and reminded her that she had replied to a letter about Lillian Hellman I had sent her a year earlier. She responded with praise for my article on the Faulkners. I wrote well, she said, but she did not believe writing about the personal lives of artists illuminated their art, and she did not think anyone's personal life was anybody else's business. As for her, she detested the idea of biography and planned to outlive as many of her biographers as possible, for she knew they would do a perfectly dreadful job on her life. Her answer to me was the same answer she gave to everyone: NO BIOGRAPHY. I was not to take it personally.

I liked the letter very much and did not take it personally. I had just read all of Gellhorn's work, had written a book proposal, and now could not stop myself from writing more about her. I had not planned an authorized biography to begin with. I was not asking for her permission to write about her. (Indeed, I have always had my doubts about how an authorized biographer can maintain an independent point of view.) I drafted a reply to Gellhorn's letter, marshaling arguments in favor of the kind of biography I thought she would like—and then I never sent the letter. For I realized that the point was not to please her but simply to write my book. As David Roberts, Jean Stafford's biographer, says: "The truest biography is not likely to please its subject."

To say that Gellhorn was not pleased is to put it mildly. She almost never granted interviews, but in the April 1988 issue of *Vogue* she took the trouble to chat with her friend Victoria Glendinning, who announced that Gellhorn was "doing her damndest to make sure there will never, ever, be a biography of Martha Gellhorn." Gellhorn then said there was an "academic kook" (me) attempting a biography anyway:

> I'm writing around asking anyone he might approach to tell him to sod off. I hate modern biographies of writers who are not public figures and not fair game. The only things biographers are interested in are your love affairs and your eccentricities. A writer should be read, not written about. I wish to retain my lifelong obscurity.

This from a woman whose glamorous photo had appeared on the cover of *Saturday Review* and on numerous book jackets, who lived a spotlighted period with Ernest Hemingway, including a filmed appearance in a Hedda Hopper documentary. *Collier's* magazine went out of its way to advertise and feature Gellhorn as their blonde and beautiful war correspondent; Eleanor Roosevelt made Gellhorn the focus of several of her "My Day" nationally syndicated newspaper columns; and Gellhorn herself fictionalized and dramatized her experience, including her "eyewitness" account of a lynching that (she confessed to Mrs. Roosevelt) she made up.

In the *Vogue* interview, Gellhorn spoke simultaneously about her "lifelong obscurity" and her status as "an historic monument." How many obscure figures have an interview published in *Vogue*? If I had any doubts about pursuing a biography of Gellhorn, they were laid to rest when I received a letter from Bill Buford, then editor of *Granta*, a curious choice to serve as Gellhorn's emissary, since Gellhorn admitted in *Vanity Fair*:

> "He did something absolutely terrible to me, and everyone thought I'd never forgive him. He simply stole something from my book, *The View from the Ground*, which was being published

in America. He claims he asked me. But when I do business, I expect a letter or something. He just pinched a part of the book and put it in the magazine. I seriously thought of killing him, but I was too busy." So she sued? "Don't be ridiculous! I called him a monster, a creep, and told everyone I'd never speak to him again. Then came the big bouquet of flowers and the abject letter of apology, full of lies of course. And I was back talking to him within three weeks."

Writing on Gellhorn's behalf, Buford expressed his dismay that I was going ahead with my biography. Didn't I know that there was an authorized biography in the works? This was news, especially since it did not square with anything Gellhorn had said about her loathing of biographies. None of the people I had interviewed had heard of an authorized biographer, and I was troubled only by the suspicion that Gellhorn might be behaving like Lillian Hellman—wanting a handpicked man or woman to write the official, uncontested version of her life. At any rate, the very suggestion that someone else might be doing a biography spurred me on.

Yet on the road to Catscradle (after I had finished a draft of the biography) I was gripped by a sense of unreality. Would I have to go home and tell my editor that I had not been able to find Gellhorn's cottage? One last stop—because we were sure that we had somehow gone past it. "No," a neighbor told Beryl, Catscradle was just ahead. The neighbor did not think anyone was at home; the car had been gone all day.

A hundred feet ahead we found the tidy white cottage, serene in its white-railed enclosure, sitting upon flat, greenish-tan ground. It was precisely the kind of quiet, modest hideaway I expected Gellhorn to own. I started taking photographs from the road. "Aren't you going to go in?" Ron asked. "I don't think there's anyone home," I almost gasped, expecting any moment that a car would pull up and Gellhorn would ask me what I was doing on her property. As we approached the cottage my wife had been giving me glances, which put the question: "What are you going to do? What will you say?"

Ron opened the gate, and I walked in. It was just like writing her biography. Once I had begun, I could not stop. I took shots from various angles and close-ups. It was getting dark, and many of the photographs, I knew, would offer only a dim view of the surroundings. I imagine that every biographer, sooner or later, has this feeling of being at once so near and yet so far away from his subject. As we drove away, I took a photograph of the road sign pointing to Kilgwrrwg, the place name Gellhorn had put at the end of *The View from the Ground*.

If there are other biographers with such stories to tell, they rarely make it into print. A rare example of a biographer's confession can be found in Joan Givner's *The Self-Portrait of a Literary Biographer*. She is the biographer of Katherine Anne Porter and Mazo de la Roche. Instead of adopting a conventional approach—showing how she became interested in her subjects, conducted her research, assembled her narrative, and came to terms with her finished product—Givner writes in a more informal and personal style, dividing her text into short numbered paragraphs. They do not follow in chronological order but rather reflect the themes of her self-portrait and her interaction with the lives she has studied—an approach that has influenced the structure of this book.

This daring method—biographers rarely reveal much about *their* personal lives—does open up and air the biographer's role in a novel way. But it is not apparent, especially at the beginning of the book, how some of the personal details of Givner's life and her family history inform her quest as a biographer. It is possible, of course, to read between the lines, and Givner is right not to spell out some of the connections between herself and her subjects, leaving some discoveries for the reader to make. Nevertheless, the best parts of her book are those sections where she engages in dialogue and correspondence with sources like Eudora Welty, who question the biographer's motives and results or encourage her efforts.

The early part of the self-portrait would have benefited from this fusion of personal and professional quests, showing perhaps in an incident how biography and autobiography, the biographer and her subject, coalesce. Givner has made a bold beginning, but other biographers will need to go beyond her in finding a form that achieves a balance that heretofore has been the province of novels taking biographers as their subjects.

In a category all to himself in this respect is Norman Mailer and his much maligned biography of Marilyn Monroe. Unlike most biographers, Mailer does not hide behind a third-person voice. In *Marilyn* he is very personal, confessing his biases, expressing his doubts about his qualifications as a biographer, yet treating Monroe as a fellow artist and positing an affinity between them—which, I have concluded—is certainly there. As I show in *The Lives of Norman Mailer*, both he and Monroe are self-invented figures and have craved public exposure and dreamed of a fame that is extra-literary, transcending the usual appeal of authors and movie stars, and aiming for nothing less than a transformation in the consciousnesses of their times.

THE GASKELL RAID on the Brontë archive, by the way, is re-
plete with the ironies that Henry James could have turned into
yet another story about the problematic nature of biography.
Patrick Brontë asked Mrs. Gaskell to become the authorized
biographer because of an anonymous piece about the family
published in *Sharpe's London Magazine.* The writing seemed
"malignant" to Charlotte's friend Ellen Nussey, who wrote to
Patrick suggesting that Mrs. Gaskell should be designated to
write a biography that would answer the misrepresentations
of such articles. As Lucasta Miller points out, however, the
offending article was virtually a word-for-word copy of Mrs.
Gaskell's long letter to a friend describing her first meeting
with Charlotte Brontë! Somehow the letter had "strayed," to
use Miller's word, into the hands of a journalist. So, in effect,
Mrs. Gaskell, who had already begun to create the Brontë
myth, was commissioned to destroy it. Patrick's letter inviting
her to write the biography is the best example I know of the
futility of authorized biography:

Finding that a great many scribblers, as well as some clever and truthful writers, have published articles in newspapers and tracts respecting my dear daughter Charlotte since her death, and seeing that many things that have been stated are untrue, but more false; and having reason to think that some may venture to write her life who will be ill-qualified for the undertaking, I can see no better plan under the circumstances than to apply to some established author to write a brief account of her life and to make some remarks on her works. You seem to me the best qualified for doing what I wish should be done.

As Lucasta Miller shows, while Mrs. Gaskell wrote a classic biography, it withheld as much as it revealed, and it has taken many generations of biographers to pry out of the "Brontë myth" the essentials of a reliable biography. The idea, in other words, that authorization is to be equated with authenticity, is a canard.

In *Cakes and Ale*, Somerset Maugham sees the humor rather than the horror in James's vision of the biographer. The second wife of Edward Driffield requests that Alroy Kear, a minor novelist, write the biography of her late husband, one of England's most distinguished writers (a fictionalized version of Thomas Hardy). Kear soon realizes that the true story of Driffield's early years cannot be told without including the story of his great love and first wife, Rosie, who calls to mind the great writer's rough beginnings, and is sure to offend the second Mrs. Driffield, who is fiercely protective of her husband's fame. A tour-de-force treatment of English literary life, the novel's inside view of the making and breaking of writers' reputations also provides insight into the opportunities and constraints of authorized biography.

Michael Foot, biographer of his friend and political hero, Aneurin Bevan, a Labour cabinet minister in the Attlee government and founder of Britain's National Health Service, revealed to me an incident in his research that is reminiscent of Kear's first-wife problem. Foot discovered that in his twenties Bevan had fallen passionately in love with and had written letters and poems to a woman who was still alive in the 1970s and who agreed to be interviewed about her relationship with Bevan. Foot wrote up the story based on the interview and on Bevan's letters, presenting the results to Bevan's formidable widow, Jennie Lee, a prominent and outspoken Labour party member and a dear friend of Foot's. Lee knew there had been other women in her husband's life. In this case the relationship the biographer described had been over for many years before Bevan married Lee. Nonetheless she advised Foot to suppress the story. "If you publish it, the press will focus on this one episode, and what you have attempted to do in the rest of the biography will be ignored." Foot accepted her advice. The press would probably sensationalize this affair, he agreed—although, as he told me, he realized that Lee wanted to be known as Bevan's only woman. She had no intention of competing for attention in a biography.

ALL EFFORTS to make distinctions between proper and improper, sanctioned and unsanctioned biography, are doomed to fail, it seems to me, for they do not address the inherent uneasiness about biography which led Boswell to call it his "presumptuous task." I once tried to level the playing field by producing a polemic for the journal *Biography*. I wanted to undercut the usual apologia that biographers present for their profession. Almost always, no matter the biographer, the defense of biography must include some acknowledgment of its invasiveness while showing how a reputable biographer ameliorates the genre's liabilities. As I bluntly put it, biographers discount the troubling meaning of their profession.

I quoted an epigraph from E. M. Forster: "I distrust Great Men. They produce a desert of uniformity around them and often a pool of blood too, and I always feel a little man's pleasure when they come a cropper." A more academic formulation might merely suggest that biography helps take the measure of great men and women.

I did not realize then that Forster's comment—his keen interest in the trajectory of lives—is at least as old as Montaigne, who remarked in one of his essays, "I have a singular curiosity . . . to pry into the souls and the natural and true opinions of the authors with whom I converse." Montaigne would certainly have been amazed at those modern literary critics who demand we isolate the writer from his work, for he continues:

> But seeing the matter preached and the preacher are different things. I would as willingly see Brutus in Plutarch, as in a book of his own. I would rather choose to be certainly informed of the confidence he had in his tent with some particular friends of his the night before a battle, than of the harangue he made the next day to his army; and of what he did in his closet and chamber, than what he did in the public square and in the senate.

Shakespeare might have been reading Montaigne when he decided to write the tent scene for *Julius Caesar*. At any rate, Montaigne's values are an affront to the modern mind, which tends to value history over biography. History makes "pleasant and easy" reading whereas Montaigne wishes to know the "variety and truth of his [man's] internal qualities, in gross and piecemeal, the diversity of means by which he is united and knit, and the accidents that threaten him." Biography and

> those that write lives, by reason they insist more upon counsels than events, more upon what sallies from within, than upon what happens without, are the most proper for my reading; and, therefore, above all others, Plutarch is the man for me. I am very sorry we have not a dozen Laertii [Diogenes Laertius, who wrote the lives of philosophers], or that he was not further extended; for I am equally curious to know the lives and for-

tunes of these great instructors of the world, as to know the diversities of their doctrines and opinions.

Plutarch did not believe it beneath the dignity of biography to relate that Pericles' son went about Athens making fun of his father's dinner table conversation. If Plutarch had as much access to gossip as we do now, I am sure he would have used it. Certainly he got Shakespeare's attention with passages about Coriolanus's childhood, which the bard whipped up into a penetrating study of a mama's boy. When it comes to vulgar biography, by the way, Shakespeare cannot be surpassed. He read Sir Thomas More's malevolent life of Richard III and exploited those details about a raunchy hunchback in a way that makes our own age seem tame indeed.

In the world of Plutarch, Sir Thomas More, Montaigne, and Shakespeare, Kitty Kelley seems far less vulgar, and more true to the spirit of biography, than my contemporaries would ever recognize. I began my polemic in *Biography* by describing my biographical cohort, so to speak:

> I belong to a group of biographers based in New York City. We call ourselves "The Biography Seminar." We meet once a month on the New York University campus, listen to an invited speaker—usually someone who has just published a biography—ask questions, offer comments, and share information. Then we adjourn for dinner and more discussion. For a biographer, the seminar is heaven. I've written five biographies and am beginning a sixth. I have also published the first annotated bibliography of writing about biography. In the seminar, I've had the opportunity to learn from and submit my work to distinguished biographers. Regardless of the month's topic, the seminar constitutes a continuous dialogue about the genre and about where biographers think they are headed.

Last year [1996] we had an unusual meeting, an open forum. In the midst of a wide-open discussion that touched on Janet Malcolm's recent attack on biographers in *The Silent Woman*, I hazarded the observation that I saw little difference between what might be called the high and low of biography, between Richard Ellmann and Kitty Kelley, for example. I was attacked on all sides. Only one seminar member thought I might be joking, deliberately provoking outrage by overstating the case. Actually I was serious, and my friends should not have been so shocked. I have been calling myself an "outlaw biographer" for years, and I was simply generalizing from my own experience in order to say, "All biographers are outlaws."

To me, the only scandalous thing about my statement was that I had never read a Kitty Kelley biography. I felt I did not need to because I maintained—and still do—that while biographies may differ in degree, they are all of a kind. Biography is one—whether you call it literary, historical, celebrity, authorized, or unauthorized. No matter what you call it, biography is the work of a scoundrel.

There is something demonic about biography; after all, the biographer is taking possession of another's soul. Kitty Kelley has become an apt target because she goes after her subjects with such relish. "It takes a real pushy pants to do it," she observed to an interviewer. She has riled not only her subjects but also her fellow biographers, provoking George Carpozi, Jr., to write a muckraking biography of *her*. She is the shame of the genre, the biographer's scourge. At least this is how the biographers I know react to her.

Then I actually read a Kitty Kelley biography. I chose *His Way: The Unauthorized Biography of Frank Sinatra*. It is the only book of hers to receive significant critical praise—from

William Safire in the *New York Times*, from Jonathan Yardley in the *Washington Post*, and from Steve Weinberg in his excellent book, *Telling the Untold Story: How Investigative Reporters Are Changing the Craft of Biography*. Even so, the Sinatra biography received mostly bad notices and was lumped together with her other work. Still, I thought it only fair to judge her by what was probably her best effort.

I found her biography impressive, especially when she lets the voices of the people she interviewed dominate scene after scene. There is very little narrative voice in Kitty Kelley, and what there is is quite pedestrian, even incompetent. She writes of one New Year's Eve in 1945—how many were there? She has Frankie spewing "hateful venom" at the press. It is nice to know that there must be a benign form of poison. One controversy rages "like a fire in an oil well, stopping only when it ran dry." Such sentences reveal that Kitty has feeble powers of analysis. (Note that like many biographers I am already on a first-name basis with my subject.) But it is the people she talks to who matter, the people who answer her questions and have stories to tell. They have wonderful stories, most of them filled with what is commonly called dirt.

That is what I like about Kitty: she serves up the raw data. It does not get blended into a bland narrative, all-wise, all-knowing voice. Instead you get a sense of all the people she interviewed. You know that some of them are exaggerating, some are lying, and some are trying to tell the truth. The stories form patterns: that Sinatra's spoiled-boy's arrogance turns vicious once he has power and money is undeniable. This is the story that Kitty wants to tell. True, she has little to say about the great voice and his art. So what? Other biographers can tackle that. What Kitty is best equipped to provide is evil because, I suspect, she is evil, and it takes one to know one. I don't think

I'm quite enough of an outlaw to take on a Sinatra—although I must say that Kitty's moxie is inspiring.

In Kitty's hands, biography is Forster's anti-heroic genre. This is why she makes many people mad and also why she is so popular. The only thing that excites readers as much as an uplifting story is one about a great fall. Biographers rarely show Kitty's relish for demolition. (An exception is Jerry Oppenheimer, Martha Stewart's unauthorized biographer, whose acknowledgments thank all those whom Martha stepped on along the way and who spoke to him.)

Biography began as elegy, panegyric, and hagiography; it has taken several centuries to bring it back to earth, and God bless Kitty Kelley for still trying. She refuses to blink at the fact that biographers are bringers of bad news, the messengers who are often shot.

Kitty has been accused of many transgressions. Here is the bill of indictment:

1. She fabricates quotations to make the stories sound better. (Thucydides did that too.)

2. She says she interviewed people who deny she did. (Well, Kitty does seem to engage in stretchers. She counts as interviews people who say to her, "No, I won't talk to you." Sometimes they say, "I won't talk to you because . . ." That kind of reply, judging by my own experience, may actually yield an important bit of information.)

3. She is sneaky. She goes along with photographers to their shoots and casually insinuates herself into conversations. (Not nice, I grant you. But I give Kitty points for her resourcefulness.)

4. She pretends she is the authorized biographer of her subjects. (If any interviewee believes that, they deserve what they

get. Anyway, I *hate* authorized biography. Who has the right to authorize the biographer's appropriation of another's life?)

5. Kitty pretends she is on the interviewee's side. She cultivates a sympathetic persona getting people to relax and say more than they intended to. (As Janet Malcolm says, every good reporter does that, and she would pretty much agree with Sinatra that the press—and biographers too—are slime. Why shouldn't Frank be mad that someone—anyone—should write up his life? How can they possibly know him as well as he knows himself? Frank, you have a point. It's just that you miss what you can't see, what no biographical subject can see: precisely those sides of yourself that are invisible to you but stick out so clearly to other people and to your biographers.)

6. Kitty does not check out her sources. She goes with stories because they are sensational, not because they are necessarily true. (I suspect that Kitty is guilty as charged. But not all stories are checkable, or checkable at the time the biographer is on the job. If the biographer presents a narrative made up almost exclusively of stories that are identified as coming from individual voices, I believe she is entitled to go with what she's got, especially if—as in the case of the Sinatra biography—the stories fit a pattern. Other biographers can correct Kitty. The best reply to one biography of Frank Sinatra is another biography of Frank Sinatra.)

7. Kitty is intolerably invasive. She purportedly had her husband root through Elizabeth Taylor's garbage cans. (This only proves my point that biography is an unsanitary occupation. There is no such thing as stooping too low for evidence. A visitor once asked William Faulkner if he could retrieve from the wastebasket a few pages the novelist had just discarded. Faulkner graciously granted the request. Literary biographers,

no less than celebrity biographers or any other kind, are on a garbage detail. It might smell better in university archives, but my hands get pretty filthy by the end of the day. They give you gloves at Boston University's Mugar Memorial Library. They think they are preserving their documents, but actually they are protecting you from their dirt.)

Kitty's sins may put her at the low end of biography, but at the high end (if you think literary biography is a high) biographers are busy practicing their genteel versions of her stratagems. Literary biographers, if they have any style at all, are confecting a narrative out of voices and letters and documents of many kinds; this narrative is obviously a construct, a kind of fiction, which like the novel can tell the truth, or aspects of the truth, but which is obviously not the life itself. But then nothing is the life itself—not even Sinatra's as he lived it minute by minute. He took his confections to market. This is why we need many biographies of the same subject: the biographers' motivations and their subjects' are always mixed. There is no purely apprehended life, and where there is no purity, there is evil, corruption.

Biographers shy away from this conclusion. They do not wish to feel tainted. They want to feel noble—that they are rescuing, rehabilitating, or burnishing the reputations of great figures. They often admire their subjects. But they do not need to; indeed, admiration may get in the way, and in some cases it is impossible. Admire Hitler? Stalin? This duo did have their admirers. But biography should not be the haunt of hagiographers. That job is always open to Sinatra's lackeys.

Not every biography needs to be muckraking. I've never written an exposé. But I'm conscious that I'm exposing parts of my subjects that they would just as soon see covered. I sympathize with their nakedness. I acknowledge their right to protest.

But I won't stop work. And I breathe easier knowing that Kitty is out their beating the bushes in front of me, making it easier for me to follow the trail.

It seems to me that biographers are just beginning to be as reckless and as dynamic as the greatest novelists; biographers are just beginning to exercise some of the creative freedom that novelists have taken for granted. The biggest mistake we (biographers) could make is to cut ourselves off from Kitty or from Janet, for that matter. Let's admit, let's even glory in the evil problematics of our genre, the better to understand and to enrich it.

NEARLY A DECADE after I wrote about Kitty Kelley, I have not changed my views about biography. But I have become curious about how to address the hostility that biography arouses. Above all, I want to examine the modern origins of the genre in the work of Dr. Johnson and his own biographer, Boswell. I am especially curious as to why no one has written a biography that even approaches the level of candor and curiosity that Boswell demonstrated in his life of Johnson and that Johnson himself practiced in his life of the poet Richard Savage.

In October 1750, Samuel Johnson published a description of biography that has never been surpassed. He wrote with a generosity and firmness that I have found lacking in other accounts of the genre. Biographers and their critics have generally treated the subject with defensiveness and hostility. Since Johnson, writing about biography has been an exercise in apologetics and skepticism. As a practicing biographer, and as a scholar of biography, I read Johnson's description as the only statement of first principles that evokes the genre's magnificent possibilities and places it at the center of the Enlightenment project. Because the modern world has subverted that project, Johnson's belief that biography provides access to the universal truths of our lives has been put down.

Johnson begins his brief for biography by observing that all joy or sorrow for the happiness or calamities of others is produced by an action of the imagination, that realises the event however fictitious, or approximates it however remote, by placing us for a time, in the condition of him whose fortune we contemplate; so that we feel, while the deception lasts, whatever motion would be excited by the same good or evil happening to ourselves.

I suppose Johnson is calling upon the faculty of empathy—the ability not only to sympathize with other human beings but also to put ourselves in their places. To understand anything about others or about the world is to feel it, Johnson suggests—or at least to imagine that we feel it. The distinction between actuality and imagination is crucial—that is, there is a difference between what really happened and what we imagined happened, yet we cannot think or feel without exercising the deception of the imagination, which is a conceit that we can be "excited by the same good or evil happening" to others as though it were happening to ourselves. In the lives of others, in other words, we read our own. Or as Johnson puts it, "we readily conform our minds" to the "parallel circumstances" and "kindred images" we find in the "narratives of the lives of particular persons." This is why he claims that "no species of writing" is "more worthy of cultivation than biography."

Johnson's embrace of biography is startling to anyone who reads reviews of biography or has a grasp of the literature about the genre. Biography is now viewed as, at best, a second rate form of writing. To the academy it is rarely viewed as scholarship; to the literary community it ranks well below the novel, for example, in importance; to the professional reviewer it is merely a story to be retold as if the reviewer wrote the biography; to organizers of writers' workshops, biography does not exist. Only general readers agree with Johnson, for year after year they continue to support the boom in biography, a boom that is clearly in evidence in the *New York Times Book Review*, which each week rarely reviews fewer than three biographies. Given the limited number of books reviewed in that influential organ, the predominance of biographies is remarkable.

I suspect general readers would second Johnson's contention that no other species of writing "can be more delightful, or more useful, none can more certainly enchain the heart by irresistible interest, or more widely diffuse instruction to every diversity of condition." Indeed, his words read like a recipe for attracting the general reader—or perhaps I should use Virginia Woolf's term, "the common reader." Her locution comes to mind when Johnson observes: "I have often thought that there has rarely passed a life of which a judicious and faithful narrative would not be useful." Every life, Johnson emphasizes, is bound by certain universals: "We are all prompted by the same motives, all deceived by the same fallacies, all animated by hope, obstructed by danger, entangled by desire, and seduced by pleasure." I have returned to Johnson again and again as I wrote my biographies because so much of the literature about biography denies his basic proposition. Reviewers constantly ask: Is this subject worthy of a biography? Or critics carp that writers do not make interesting subjects. Nothing happens in their lives but their writing. Johnson confronted the same prejudices: "It is frequently objected to relations of particular lives," he noted, "that they are not distinguished by any striking or wonderful vicissitudes." But this desire for dramatic incident is prompted, Johnson retorted, by "false measures of excellence and dignity." Biographers should "eradicate" such prejudices by passing "slightly over those performances and incidents, which produced vulgar greatness, to lead the thoughts into domestick privacies, and display the minute details of daily life, where exterior appendages are cast aside, and men excel each other only by prudence and by virtue."

Johnson argued for a vision of biography that took an intrinsic interest in the individual. By that standard, almost any detail might prove revelatory, Johnson insisted: "Thus Salust, the great master, has not forgot, in his account of Catiline, to remark that his walk was now quick, and again slow, as an indication of a mind revolving something with violent commotion."

Johnson's own biographer took up his call for an attention to "minute details." But both in Boswell's time and in ours, a fair number of critics have dismissed the details as trivial and even demeaning. Indeed, there has never been a time since Johnson's essay when his view of biography has reigned. On the contrary, John Gibson Lockhart, Sir Walter Scott's biographer, deliberately rejected Boswell's dipping into "domestick privacies" and "minute details." The nineteenth century proved to be a disaster for biography, from which the genre has yet to recover. Although there is much palaver in the press about the candor of biography and its exposure of public lives, no biographer has dared to come near the kind of intimacy Johnson favored and Boswell practiced.

The contemporary biographer faces a series of roadblocks and traffic checks. Reviewers police contemporary biography, looking for those minute details that, they say, don't contribute to an understanding of the author's work or of the public figure's career. In place of Johnson's universalizing of human lives, moderns have compartmentalized biography. The typical review tells us that we don't need to know this, that, or the other about the biographical subject. Certain biographies buy into this form of segregation as well. I remember one of my colleagues explaining to me that he did not tell the story of Dwight Macdonald's affairs with his students because they had nothing to do with his significance as a critic. "Then, sir," I can hear Samuel Johnson say, "you are not writing biography." Similarly, Susan Sontag announces in *Under the Sign of Saturn* the modernist credo: "One cannot use the life to interpret the work. But one can use the work to interpret the life." Johnson, I submit, would regard such statements as nonsense. The life and the work, the imagination and actuality, flow into each other all the time.

Jenny Uglow, a biographer of Mrs. Gaskell, complained in a review of my Rebecca West biography that I spent as much time on West's affair with the Nuremberg prosecutor Francis Biddle as on the trials themselves, which West wrote about for the *New Yorker*. So I did because the poignancy of her affair with Biddle filled her letters at the time, whereas readers can easily read her Nuremberg articles (collected in *A Train of Powder*). I was fascinated with the rhythm of her life at that period, which she herself saw as her last great romance. That I did not give the trials more space did not mean I took no interest in them—indeed I would later publish an article on the way West, Janet Flanner, and Martha Gellhorn reported Nuremberg. But for the purposes of a biography it was the person in the writer who commanded my full attention.

Statements like Sontag's consign biography to the ghetto of modernism. Biographies that dwell on the person as much as the work are now routinely labeled pathographies, though the biography to which Oates applied the term has to account for fully a third of Jean Stafford's life as a record of disability. It seems to me that the third of the biography that charts her long decline got the proportions of Stafford's life just about right. Stafford's writer's block is as significant in a biography as her literary achievement.

Johnson certainly believed that biography did more than pay homage to achievement. He wrote: "More knowledge may be gained of a man's real character, by a short conversation with one of his servants, than from a formal and studied narrative, begun with his pedigree, and ended with his funeral." I took his words to heart when I interviewed Rebecca West's hairdresser, and it is one of my great regrets that the man who cleaned Susan Sontag's apartment would not speak to me. I find it interesting, by the way, that it was a man.

To admit of such an interest in Susan Sontag's housekeeping is considered scandalous by those who treat literary figures and literature as somehow detachable from the life that everyone else lives. What I like about biography is that it is a great leveler. The high and the low, the great and the small, make their beds and sleep in them. There is no doubt, especially with living subjects, that the biographer is invading their privacy. Johnson understood the problem of treading on the sensibilities of the "many who think it an act of piety to hide the faults or fails of their friends, even when they can no longer suffer by their detection." But like a devoted biographer, he remained loyal to the work of biography, which meant that he opposed censorship. In the following passage he is not speaking specifically of biographies of living figures, but he might as well be, for he addresses the issue of when it is proper to write a biography and why it is necessary to write biographies sooner rather than later (the later, I would add, will take care of itself):

> If a life [the writing of a life] be delayed till all interest and
> envy are at an end, and all motive to calumny or flattery are

suppressed, we may hope for impartiality, but must expect little intelligence; for the incidents which give excellence to biography are of a volatile and evanescent kind, such as soon
escape the memory, and are rarely transmitted by tradition.

When biographies are delayed, not only does the data disap-
pear, the attitude toward the subject changes, and it becomes
very difficult for the biographer to recapture exactly how the
subject's contemporaries regarded the subject while she or he
was alive. While revising my biography of Gellhorn shortly
after her death, I could see the difference already. There is a
subtle relaxing of attitudes, a subsidence of tension that ac-
companies the biographical subject's demise. The later biography may seem more impartial, but that is partly a function
of distance, not necessarily of greater knowledge. To see how
history and biography can dilute as well as broaden an understanding of the biographical subject, one only needs to read
William Faulkner's great historiographical novel *Absalom,
Absalom!*, in which each new generation of narrators creates
a less impassioned, if more objective and complex, view of
Thomas Sutpen.

My biographies of Marilyn Monroe, Lillian Hellman, and
Rebecca West were begun after my subjects had died, and there
was not a day I did not regret not having had access to the living person, to watch for those gestures and mannerisms that
make up an individual. Although I had ten thousand Rebecca
West letters and many other papers to draw on, as well as a biography of West by Victoria Glendinning, I would have given
up a portion of them just to have had the opportunity to observe West as I observed Susan Sontag on many occasions. My
biographies of Martha Gellhorn, Norman Mailer, and Susan
Sontag were written without their cooperation, and I did not

have access to their archives, but I felt a proximity to them that stimulated an act of the imagination. In Gellhorn's case, I was extremely fortunate to interview her high school classmates— most of whom were dead by the time my book was published. Gellhorn's authorized biographer did not do a thorough job. She failed to consult my archive of recorded interviews and correspondence at the University of Tulsa, either because she is an inept researcher or realized that using my material would have angered the Gellhorn estate.

But I am not arguing on Johnsonian principles for the superiority of writing the biography while the subject is alive. To be sure, the biographer of a living figure faces considerable obstacles—not the least of which are gaps in the evidence and the silence of witnesses—problems I have had to confront in my own work. Rather, I want to rectify the idea that the biographer of a living figure labors under insurmountable disadvantages. John Lukacs notes in *The Hitler of History* that one of the best biographies of Adolf Hitler was published in 1935. And Herbert Butterfield argued long ago in *George III and the Historians* that the material of contemporary biographies of the king were an important element in later biographies and would remain so.

The aggrieved tone of so many reviews of contemporary biography triggers Johnson's riposte: "If there is a regard due to the memory of the dead, there is yet more respect to be paid to knowledge, to virtue, and to truth."

What continues to fascinate me as a biographer and as an assiduous reader of contemporary reviews is how they reject Johnson's certainty that biography is a first-rate genre with its own form of justification. His point that any life is worth a biography is one that few of my contemporaries seem to embrace unless they are reading novels. Johnson's *Life of Savage* comes to mind as a way to test his theory and practice against the contemporary response to biography.

To the contemporary biographer, the *Life of Savage* ought to be a marvel. At the outset, Johnson proceeds with a confidence in the value of his work that is bracing. That he is dealing with a minor poet matters not at all, for he is untroubled by notions of what a literary biography should be. All biography is one, he implies. Here is a writer who need not worry about Chief Inspector Malcolm's apprehension of biographical burglars or Coroner Oates's inquests into pathography. On the contrary, Johnson observes, "The heroes of literary as well as civil history have been very often no less remarkable for what they have suffered than for what they have achieved."

I will not rehearse the familiar details of Savage's life, except to say that I regard Johnson's attack on the Countess of Macclesfield, Savage's alleged mother, with considerable envy. She was still alive when Johnson published his biography. No present-day biographer, especially in England, would dare to write so frankly for fear of a libel suit. Undoubtedly today's reviewers would castigate Johnson as too "judgmental" and cruel.

Johnson understood Savage's faults and did not minimize them, though he invented a language for his hero's transgressions that maintains his empathy for his subject while showing the reader why others might feel otherwise. Thus Johnson strikes a regretful tone: "It must be confessed that Mr Savage's esteem was no very certain possession, and that he would lampoon at one time those whom he had praised at another." Similarly, of Savage's brief, atrocious career as an actor, Johnson deems the theater "a province for which nature seemed not to have designed him." Savage's fitful personality, his winning and losing ways, are embedded in Johnson's perfectly balanced sentences: "It was his peculiar happiness, that he scarcely ever found a stranger, which he did not leave a friend; but it must likewise be added, that he had not often a friend long, without obliging him to become a stranger." The seesaw of Savage's life is preserved in these stately sentences, which give the biography a decorum and dignity that its subject seldom sustained.

Nearly always a trial to himself and to everyone else, Savage nevertheless succeeds as the subject of a biography because Johnson shows just how much energy Savage invested in his complaints. Not much of Savage's poetry is quoted, but as Johnson signals at the beginning of the biography, it is the agony of the man, not the work of the poet, that deeply engages the biographer's imagination. It was the labor of Savage's life to broadcast how greatly he suffered, and Johnson does justice to that misery, which he identifies in a brilliant phrase as arising from his subject's "gaiety of imagination." Today I suppose we would call such a man paranoid, and that word reveals how constrained, how clinical, biography has become. According to the Oxford English Dictionary, "paranoia" is not employed in public discourse before the year 1892; it is then used to designate delusions of persecution. Certainly the definition fits Savage, but how fortunate that Johnson did not have that word to put into his own dictionary. For such terms rob a life of its uniqueness, or at least the illusion of uniqueness, upon which all biography is based. In other words, in Johnson's biography Savage suffers exuberantly, gloriously, and sometimes sordidly, but always in his own savage way.

Nowadays biographies are typed. A reviewer calls Peter Conradi's life of Iris Murdoch a "department store biography." Never mind what that term might mean; the point is that biography gets quickly slotted and categorized and cannot be regarded as the precious, exceptional story Johnson had to tell. Or so it seems if one reads only the words of the scornful reviewers and critics. The actual readers of biography apparently feel otherwise, judging by the letters from them I have received and the popularity of the genre. Indeed, readers (reviewers are seldom readers) speak with an eighteenth-century enthusiasm for biography, an involvement with the trajectory and contingency of lives that Johnson captures in his tripartite division of Savage's biography—from its blighted beginning to its momentary triumph and its ultimate defeat:

> So peculiar were the misfortunes of this man, deprived of an estate and title by a particular law, exposed and abandoned by a mother, defrauded by a mother of a fortune which his father had allotted him, he entered the world without a friend; and though his abilities forced themselves into esteem and reputation, he was never able to obtain any real advantage, and whatever prospects arose were always intercepted as he began to approach them.

Savage's failure is apparent, no matter where one puts the blame. But for Johnson it is the story of the life that matters, and the quality of that story, rather than a life that can be abstracted from the biography and assessed. Thus the biographer concludes: "Those are no proper judges of his conduct, who have slumbered away their time on the down of plenty; nor will any wise man presume to say, 'Had I been in Savage's condition, I should have lived or written better than Savage.'" What matters, Johnson emphasizes, is "this relation" (the story the biography has to tell), and this relation, in Johnson's last words,

> will not be wholly without its use, if those, who languish under any part of his sufferings, shall be enabled to fortify their patience, by reflecting that they feel only those afflictions from which the abilities of Savage did not exempt him; or those, who

in confidence of superior capacities or attainments, disregard the common maxims of life, shall be reminded, that nothing will supply the want of prudence; and that negligence and ir-regularity, long continued, will make knowledge useless, wit ridiculous, and genius contemptible.

To the contemporary biographer, Johnson's direct address to his audience and his imagining the reader's state of mind, char-acter, and position in life are intriguing. For each kind of reader he has a word—a warning really—that only by em-pathizing with Savage can they understand the nature of his life. Only Savage had the genius to be Savage, and readers must cross the divide of personality, place, and position that separates them from his life.

The Enlightenment conclusion to the *Life of Savage*, it seems to me, is the opposite of what one might term romantic biography—in which the biographer projects himself into the life of his subject, so that biography becomes autobiography, and the biographer gravitates precisely to what he shares in common with his subject. I am drawn to this distinction be-tween the Enlightenment and the romantic biographer be-cause there is another contemporary biographer who has shown considerable interest in the *Life of Savage*.

In *Dr. Johnson and Mr. Savage*, Richard Holmes, author of distinguished biographies of Shelley and Coleridge, and of studies of the biographer's method (*Footsteps* and *Sidetracks*), continues his discussion of biography as a romantic form. He believes that the rise of biography as both a popular and seri-ous genre in the eighteenth century heralded the advent of ro-manticism, a literary movement that prized the truth to be plumbed in the self. The poet turned inward, abandoning the standards of the neoclassical age (which elevated reason as the measure of things), and sought truth through individual experience, priding himself on the use of his imagination and often challenging the norms and strictures of the status quo.

Holmes concedes that the august Dr. Johnson is a strange figure to put forward as a harbinger of romanticism. Johnson, an opponent of the American Revolution, sympathetic to the Jacobite cause, and a devoutly religious man, hardly seems the prototype of a romantic writer. But this Johnson is Boswell's historical effigy, Holmes contends. Thirty years younger than his subject, Boswell craved the guidance of an all-wise mentor. The erratic biographer, lacking in discipline, saw in Johnson a steadying father figure and exaggerated those elements of Johnson's character that suited Boswell's needs. Holmes shows that Boswell consistently muted Johnson's insecure feelings, disputing or ignoring sources that revealed Johnson's immaturity and sexual needs.

Holmes portrays Johnson as an ungainly, hulking figure—subject to fits of depression and violent nervous outbreaks of emotion. He failed several times as a schoolmaster, often frightening his pupils with his temper and with a grotesque physical appearance caused by the scrofula he suffered as a child. Sexually frustrated, he pursued a number of well-born ladies—his princesses, as Holmes calls them. Johnson did not come into his own as a man or achieve success as a literary figure until his middle age, after struggling for several years in London. This is the Johnson who emerges from Holmes's narrative—a passionate but uncertain man who only gradually learned to subdue his demons.

Holmes's insistence on this more vulnerable and unpredictable Dr. Johnson helps him explain Johnson's fascination with Savage, who becomes, Holmes alleges, Johnson's other unreliable half. As Holmes admits, the title of his book alludes to another key text in romanticism, *Dr. Jekyll and Mr. Hyde*. Savage is, in short, Johnson's dark, uncontrollable double.

Holmes carefully explores Johnson's first years in London, and how Johnson came to know Savage at precisely the moment Johnson was seeking to establish his literary voice. In their long walks through London streets, Savage indoctrinated Johnson into the lore of literary London and impressed upon him the powerful myth of the forlorn and isolated poet, doomed to walk alone because he had offended the higher powers of society by speaking his unbridled mind. Such talk appealed to the young, struggling Sam Johnson, who could well believe that the mesmerizing Savage was a kind of fallen literary angel.

Holmes presents a vivid story, yet one is taken aback when he admits there is not a single scrap of evidence that describes the two men together. Johnson and Savage had mutual friends, yet no description of the two writers together has come to light. Holmes seems infected by the romanticism he studies. He inclines to delving in inferences and creating an atmosphere that is downright novelistic. Romantics are great questers; they like to work up a great air of anticipation and revelation. By this measure, Holmes does not disappoint. He has written a provocative and even a thrilling book.

Yet *Dr. Johnson and Mr. Savage* may also be a misguided book. For me, Johnson is worthy of biographer's attention today precisely because he emphasizes the effort we must make to overcome ourselves and empathize with others. He may indeed have shared certain qualities with Savage, but for both Johnson and the audience he directly addresses in the biography's conclusion, the overcoming of differences is what leads to an understanding of the biographical subject. Is it merely neoclassical decorum that prompts Johnson not to specify the nature of his friendship with Savage? Or does he—as I think likely, given his statements of biographical principle—realize that to invoke his own sensibility would mean engaging in self-indulgence and special pleading? Johnson did not write literary biography as we know it today; I believe he would have found it too constraining, since he would have considered the debates about how to balance the life and the work narrow-minded. A biography, in his view, appeals to several different audiences at once, and a biography's prose must move between different audience levels—sometimes even within a sentence.

The legacy of Johnson's *Life of Savage* is its language, which evokes and mimics the rocking back and forth of its subject's fortunes. Johnson broods on the nexus of character and fate, on the obstacles placed in Savage's way, on the obstacles he placed in his own way, and on the audience Savage managed to gather as witness to his suffering. *The Life of Savage* cannot be reduced, in other words, to the work of one literary man obsessed with a literary alter ego. This may well be a strand of Johnson's biography, but it cannot stand for the whole, or even as a primary motivation for writing the book.

Undoubtedly Johnson did see certain parallels between his life and Savage's. But these parallels, he pointed out in his essay on biography, are "produced by an action of the imagination," which seeks to "conform our minds" to the "parallel circumstances" and "kindred images" in the "narratives of the lives of particular persons." As a reader and writer of biographies, I like his choice of the word "conform." It suggests a disciplined effort to suit our sensibility to another's, to move beyond the self, and that is why Johnson claimed that "no species of writing" is "more worthy of cultivation than biography."

8

I HAVE REPEATED Johnson's definition of the biographer's imagination—really *our* imagination as we read biography—because I want it to serve as a kind of mantra for this book. Biography as bloodsport suggests that the biographer is a combatant whom critics are charged with monitoring—and sometimes punishing. Biography as bloodsport suggests that biographers are at war with their subjects. Biography as bloodsport obliterates the idea that the discipline of biography is an Enlightenment project still worth pursuing.

What intrigues me is why the literary community early on lost faith in Johnson's Enlightenment project even as Boswell brought it to fruition. I am enough of a Hegelian to suspect that during Johnson's own time his theory and practice—as carried on and modified by Boswell—contained the seeds of its own destruction, the kernel, as it were, of its antithesis, the anti-biography mentality that biographers continued to struggle against to this day.

At this point I sense the spirit of Richard Ellmann, James Joyce's biographer, hovering over these pages. His presence overshadows this book because I have been able to read his papers, now housed in the McFarlin Library at the University of Tulsa. Although even those most hostile to biography often accord him an honorable mention, and although he never endured the animosity that biographers like me have experienced, for all that Ellmann and I are in the same boat.

Among his papers (and I will quote only from his papers in this book) I find an essay on biography that begins with a paraphrase of Wilde's statement that "every great man has his disciples, and that it is usually Judas who writes the biography." Noting Joyce's similar view of biography, Ellmann adds: "Some hostility between subjects and agents of biography is understandable; there is a sense in which the biography is necessarily invasive." He finds it perfectly understandable that T. S. Eliot and George Orwell forbade biographies of themselves. Biographers, however well intentioned, introduce an "alien point of view," Ellmann acknowledges, "something necessarily different from that mixture of self-recrimination and self-justification which accounts for a good deal of our conversation with ourselves."

But, of course, as a biographer, Ellmann cannot leave it there. He speaks for me when he suggests that "biographical invasion is warranted because the sense of ourselves which we have in isolation is to a large extent fabricated, an ennoblement or a debasement." In dialogue with ourselves we can be more heroic than others see us—or less. Then Ellmann makes a crucial distinction: autobiography is solitary; biography is social. The biographer "represents the outside world, the social self is the real self, the self only comes to exist when juxtaposed with other people."

The trouble for modern biographers, Ellmann explains, arises over the vexed concern with privacy—an issue that

Boswell, for example, did not have to confront. Or so Ellmann thinks, for he calls Boswell's book "decorous," and he observes that Boswell's idea of privacy had to do with showing Johnson among his fellows. It is a social view of "domestic privacies," which reveals that "prudence and virtue may appear more conspicuously there than in incidents of vulgar greatness." Boswell does not take into account a view of privacy that would enter the recesses of the bedroom, for example, where Johnson in a state of undress would lose the sense of propriety he always exhibits in Boswell's biography. Ellmann concludes: "Today we want to see our great men at their worst as well as their best."

I have to wonder how fresh Ellmann's reading of Boswell was when he wrote these words. Boswell certainly thought he was showing Johnson at his best and at his worst. When one of Johnson's friends petitioned Boswell to soften the harsher sides of Johnson's character, to "mitigate some of his asperities," the biographer replied that "he would not cut his claws, nor make a tiger a cat, to please anybody." The words sound like the irascible Johnson himself.

And Boswell does not simply show his subject in social interactions. He dwells, for example, on Johnson's spastic movements, his noisy eating habits, his talking to himself, his slovenly dress—including descriptions of a wig that was too small for the great man's head and stockings that drooped around his ankles. In this respect Boswell is no different from the Richard Ellmann who wrote to one of James Joyce's friends: "I am interested in any details about Joyce, no matter how seemingly trivial—his appearance, habits, speech, teaching methods; anecdotes about him; what he said about people, things, events; and the like." The biographer's obsession with his subject is aptly summed up in this sentence Ellmann wrote to a prospective interviewee who responded that he felt he had little to contribute to the biography. Any detail would be appreciated, Ellmann assured him: "I hope you will not think it absurd in a biography of Joyce to be as much interested in Joyce as Joyce was in Bloom."

Boswell's technique shocked eighteenth-century readers. Even before publishing his life of Johnson, the biographer had outraged the literary community by reporting so many of Johnson's private remarks in his book on their tour of the Hebrides. Edmund Burke, a mutual friend of Johnson and Boswell's, was shocked to read Johnson's remark that he had never heard Burke tell a good joke. So widespread was the animus against Boswell that the poet William Mason wisecracked that he was "very angry" because Johnson had not attacked him in Boswell's book. "It looks," Mason observed, "as if one was nobody." Another contemporary, John Wilks, called Boswell a dangerous man because he wrote down conversations. Wilks may have been joking—as Adam Sisman supposes in *Boswell's Presumptuous Task*—but there was an edge to the humor.

Ellmann's version of a genteel Boswell—as viewed by the twentieth-century biographer—seems ahistorical to me. Boswell was a boundary breaker and wrote biography in a world that was every bit as rough and tumble as our own, and perhaps more so. The Reverend Dr. Vicesimus Knox, the Michiko Kakutani of his day and "an essayist second in popularity only to Johnson himself," according to Adam Sisman, concluded: "Biography is every day descending from its dignity. Instead of an instructive recital, it is becoming an instrument to the mere gratification of an impertinent, not to say a malignant, curiosity." Consequently "the custom of exposing the nakedness of eminent men of every type will have an unfavourable influence on virtue. It may teach men to fear celebrity."

Biographers have to get their hands dirty. They need to get into the gore and guts of their subject. It amazed me to hear a biographer of Marianne Moore say he did no interviews for his book. When asked why, he replied: "Oh, they're so messy." Similarly, I was astounded when Ian Kershaw, one of Hitler's recent biographers, dismissed the idea of talking with the remaining men and women who were part of his subject's staff. Kershaw said he had no time to listen to their trite reminiscences. No doubt much of what he would have heard would be redundant and trivial, but I'm with Ellmann—always in search of that telling detail.

Boswell may not have believed that the bedchamber was the province of biography, but it would not have been because he thought such private worlds were off limits or insignificant. It was more a matter of what the traffic would bear—what he could get away with. When Elizabeth Desmoulin told him about how Johnson's wife spurned his sexual advances, Boswell was all ears. What did Johnson do? He kissed and fondled Desmoulin. But then, in an obvious state of arousal, he would cry, "Get you gone." The incident was important because Johnson was a devout, indeed a God-fearing, man and took sin seriously. Boswell noted in his diary: "That he should bring himself to the very verge of what he thought was a crime." Boswell suppressed the story only because it was "too delicate," by which I take to mean that revealing it in print would have jeopardized his own reputation as a biographer. There is, in fact, nothing to suggest in Boswell's behavior as a man or a biographer that he found Johnson's behavior disgusting or unfit to discuss. We know he discussed the episode with Edmund Burke. Rather it was the constraints on what was deemed proper for a biographer that held him back. As it was, he had transgressed as much as he dared.

Sisman believes that Boswell was protecting Johnson. I doubt it. More likely he was thinking of himself. In my view, it was a question of the biographer's credibility. He did not wish to jeopardize a whole biography for the sake of a single story. Biographers make trade-offs like this every day. When I was researching my biography of Rebecca West, I discovered her account of child molestation—a graphic scene in which her father stuck his penis through the slats of her crib. Psychoanalysis had brought this latent memory to consciousness, or so West thought at a time when her view of her father was particularly hostile. Later in life, as her memories of her father softened, she repudiated the memory as a fantasy. In Victoria Glendinning's biography, this episode is told in a short paragraph that is so murky and euphemistic that I doubt readers would understand what happened. I told the story in full, and wouldn't you know it? A reviewer accused me of dwelling on such incidents in order to sensationalize my biography and boost sales. In the case of literary biography, such revelations rarely result in monetary payoff. In my case, the Rebecca West biography sold about three thousand copies and not many more in Britain. It is no way to make a living.

Johnson and Boswell tacitly recognized that there would be biographers who would go beyond their definition of domestic privacies. Otherwise Boswell would not have suppressed certain negative information he had about Johnson, and Johnson would not have burned some of his papers. Both men, in other words, understood what a prying lot biographers are.

If Boswell were alive today, the insatiably curious biographer—at one point Johnson tells his pestering friend he is no longer behaving like a gentleman—would have relished the contemporary task of penetrating further into his subject's life. It will not do to confine him to an eighteenth-century chamber. A term like "domestic privacies" is as elastic as certain clauses of the U.S. Constitution. What we mean by privacy today is not precisely the same as what people in the eighteenth century meant; what person today would want to be confined to the eighteenth-century definition of the word? Boswell, that gadabout and ambitious swell, would certainly have wanted to compete with today's biographers. One cannot consign him to a decorous past.

LIKE MOST BIOGRAPHERS, Ellmann never said as much in his published writings about his methods as a biographer or about his attitude toward biography's invasiveness as he revealed in his private correspondence. In public—even in social settings—he was circumspect and cagey. An *Observer* profile of Ellmann adverted to his "easy, friendly, prosaic manner." Roger Lewis, an Ellmann student, reveals this side of the Master in *Anthony Burgess: A Biography*. The soft-spoken and diplomatic Ellmann evades jousting with the jocular novelist: "Tell me, Dick, which white wine did Joyce drink?" Burgess asks. "People come to blows over that," replies the elusive Ellmann.

A different Ellmann appears in a letter to a friend about Joycelyn Baines's biography of Joseph Conrad. Ellmann found the book fascinating but also puzzling. Why did the biographer so resolutely exclude gossip? Not even Jessie Conrad's version of Conrad's marriage proposal was admitted into the narrative because, in Baines's view, it was merely "picturesque." To Ellmann, however, her words rang true.

The biographer has to include intimate material, he emphasized, though he admired the biographer's "careful and inhibiting honesty."

Ellmann also wondered why Leon Edel indulged in facile Freudianism while deploring any mention of gossip about Henry James. Ellmann enjoyed the give-and-take of interviews and brushed aside Hugh Kenner's criticism that he relied too heavily on the spoken word. Ellmann thought to the contrary—that biographers gave too much credence to the written word. So he nagged away at interviewees, all the while pretending not to nag.

Ellmann wrote as least five politely pestering letters to J. F. Byrne, a Joyce friend and one of those infuriating sources who tell biographers he has secrets he does not wish to divulge. Byrne even tortured Ellmann by citing page numbers of passages in his memoir that hinted at "some things that one simply cannot talk about." The ever-patient Ellmann replied that what he wanted to ask would result in no "breach of confidence." Finally, with the begging ritual completed to Byrne's satisfaction, he relented and gave up the goods—but only because Ellmann was a "gentleman."

Ellmann's technique is revealed in a letter to him from Adaline Glasheen, advising him how to handle Helen Joyce, who was already fond of "nice" and "knowing" Mr. Ellmann. He had a manner that put Helen at ease. Glasheen doubted Helen really had much to tell the biographer, but she begged him, nevertheless, "for the sake of pure simple human kindness," to write to Helen with a few more questions about Joyce's personal characteristics such as his voice or the color of his hair. It would be helpful as well, Glasheen advised, to make Helen "just a little important" in no more than a paragraph. Helen, it seems, felt neglected, for she told Adaline: "The most they ever say about me is 'Giorgio married a rich American girl who was one of the best-dressed women in France.' Adaline, is that all I am? Do you think it is?"

Glasheen assessed Ellmann's finished product with considerable shrewdness and amusement. She found his literary criticism first rate, but that was also a problem, given his circumspect role as biographer, the "poker-faced presenter of information received." She understood why he adopted such a retiring pose, but she longed for him to "step out boldly to characterize Byrne or Maria Jolas or Helen Joyce. My goodness yes—who could? I do think, though, since you've met all these people in Joyce's circle you ought to leave in a sealed enveloped true descriptions for the future." I'm still looking for that sealed envelope.

I savor Glasheen's response after reading all the encomiums of Ellmann, pointing out how nonjudgmental he is and how he just presents Joyce for us to make of him what we will. To be sure. But the biographer is making a virtue of necessity. All the circumspect Ellmann would say to Glasheen's provocation was "The Joyce biographer's life is getting too complicated for any more or less human being."

Even the cautious Ellmann, however, suffered rebuke when he published James Joyce's graphic love letters to his wife Nora. The novelist Kay Boyle, one of Ellmann's sources for the Joyce biography, wrote to him: "This was an affront not only to Joyce the man, but to the privacy—and, yes, to the dignity—of all of us. What purpose it served I am unable to determine." Ellmann's frustration—one that most biographers experience, however much or little they reveal about their subjects' privacy—is evident in his reply. He regretted that they differed on what merited publication. Ellmann believed he was following Joyce's view that "we are all very imperfect beings and that it is better that this be acknowledged and even specified than not." He did not believe the letters diminished Joyce's reputation in the slightest. He conceded that he had been troubled for years about whether to publish the correspondence, but in the end he wanted to show Joyce in the full context of his life. The letters demonstrated "how carefully controlled the book *Ulysses* was."

Was Ellmann deceiving himself, or just telling Boyle less than he actually understood? There is all the difference in the world between showing human beings warts and all in a novel and doing the same in a biography. The latter work of literature will get the biographer in trouble, and would have gotten Ellmann in trouble with Joyce, I would bet, if Joyce had been alive. Literary history is littered with the wreckage of biographies that have deigned to probe too deeply into the literary personage's life. As I write, a publisher has canceled publication of a biography of Nadine Gordimer because she has objected to certain passages about her. This is a biography that enjoyed her cooperation until the biographer presented a view of his subject that she could not accept.

Ellmann was a great one for "full context." He objected to the way Leon Edel's Henry James biography quoted only phrases and a few sentences of his subject's letters—as if the biographer, once more, were cutting up his subject. As early as March 1963, more than twenty years before the letters to Nora were published, Ellmann was urging their publication to Peter du Sautoy, vice chairman of Faber and Faber. The biographer did not wish to censor Joyce. If the letters were held back, someday they would have to be done again anyway, he pointed out to the publisher. After an initial flurry of negative press, the letters would be recognized as "one of the most interesting literary and psychological documents ever published." Otherwise "we shall go down in literary history as the Mrs. Grundys of modern literature."

Ellmann received in reply what every biographer dreads: "I am against censorship and think people should be free to write and publish whatever they like," the publisher argued. "But the corollary of that is that they should be free not to publish as well. I don't think this is prudery at all, perhaps one might call it humanity." Ellmann could not be shamed, though. He replied that he thought it more humane to reveal the whole man, both his coarse and his tender sides.

In 1976, a dozen years after the exchange with Peter du Sautoy, Ellmann continued to agonize over publication of the Joyce/Nora letters. He asked his colleague Harry Levin if the letters were "so disgusting?" Was it just that Ellmann had perused them so many times that he found them inoffensive? Didn't the letters show Joyce breaking down barriers, indulging in polymorphous appetites that remained unspeakable "even in this age"? I don't have Levin's letter to Ellmann, but judging from Ellmann's words, Levin seemed to have been making a distinction between contextualized sex in his [Joyce's] books and the fierce yet random sexuality of these letters." I sympathize with Ellmann's desire to reveal Joyce fully, but again the idea that Joyce in his private letters was conducting some kind of sexual enlightenment campaign seems far-fetched, to say the least. Ellmann is trying to wrap himself in the Joycean mantle to justify what he wants to do as a biographer. In doing so, he simply delays the day when biographers will be more candid about their "presumptuous task."

10

AFTER PUBLICATION of the Joyce biography in 1959, Ellmann went looking for another subject. He thought of Faulkner, until a letter from Joseph Blotner announced that he had been chosen as the writer's authorized biographer. This would not stop some biographers from going ahead, but Ellmann's "taste for the enterprise" diminished: "Blotner is younger, and to be a middle-aged poacher upon the young seems an especially invidious position," he wrote Ben Huebsch, one of publishing's old hands.

Robert Frost turned Ellmann down, not wanting to submit to interviews. Sonia Orwell doubted an American like Ellmann could properly do her husband George. Ellmann was also too young and had not lived through the Spanish Civil War period. To the publisher William Jovanovich, Ellmann countered: "Sonia Orwell's letter assumes that Americans were detached from the Spanish Civil War, but we have passed out our petitions too, and my sense of disqualification does not come from an admission of unawareness or indifferences which she seems to regard as American." In truth, though, he did not feel "compulsive enough" about the subject, he confided to the writer Mark Harris.

Compulsion, in other words, could override a great many objections to doing a biography. Jovanovich kept scouting subjects for Ellmann, who had to tell him he had already considered Ezra Pound, but Pound has not been encouraging, and now did not seem the right time to approach the aging and frail poet. What I find fascinating about this search for a subject is that it shows not the scholar so much as the biographer with an appetite, the biographer who is looking for a victim to devour.

If I seem to be reading too much into the gentlemanly Mr. Ellmann's conduct, consider the following letter written while he was at work on his biography of Yeats. Ellmann speaks of his subject "resisting" him and of how Ellmann has "hounded him into the marriage chamber." The literary critic, reading Yeats's diaries, gives way to the "vampire intimacy" of the biographer, making it difficult to resume a "hard critical mood." The bloodthirstiness continues three days later in a letter to another friend: "I shall hound him into his grave in a month or so. If there be suicide after death, I've no doubt he's committing it, for I have introduced myself into his body—o shades of Sodom." Clearly, Ellmann relishes his role as biographer-hound. To my delight, he also expresses that sense of friction between biographer and subject that I have always felt is part of the machinery of biography.

Of course, Ellmann never seemed predatory to others. *Au contraire.* As one correspondent observed, "You always make your work sound like good luck with people cooperating—surely not so, is it?" Like all biographers, Ellmann experienced his share of rejections: "Answering your letter of July the 14th [1955], regarding my recollections of Mr. James Joyce," wrote the novelist Djuna Barnes, "I am very sorry, but for the past many years I have made it a practice never to write such notes."

Like most biographers, Ellmann could not let his own feelings show while dealing with his interviewees, although he gave away the game in a letter about his tightrope walking between Maude Gonne and her daughter, both of whom he disliked. Ellmann, a World War II veteran, mentioned the family's pro-German feelings. Maud, he reported, was not very intelligent. "Some day I'll tell you the whole story of that family, worthy of Balzac," he concluded.

The careful Ellmann rarely exposed himself to direct attack from his interviewees. I found a rare example of a slightly wounded biographer writing to Carola Giedion-Welcker, a Zurich friend of Joyce's. She was angry that he had published a few sentences she had objected to. He points out that she had sent her corrections without an explanation to his publisher, who had then forwarded her letter to him. Did she think he could just drop those sentences from his carefully constructed book? They had known each other for eight years, Ellmann reminded her, and she had had his draft for two of those. Surely the right thing would have been to address him directly. Anyway, what harm could be done to their friendship by two sentences in the context of the thirty thousand he had written? The noble Ellmann concluded, however, by assuring her, "I shall always think of you with esteem."

Of course, like a true biographer, Ellmann was really just thinking of himself. To see two sentences in print attributed to you that put you in a bad light is enough. What do you care about the other thirty thousand? Ellmann's tough side comes through here, but also his desire to put himself in the right. Does his interviewee's behavior justify his keeping those two sentences? Isn't it, rather, that Ellmann believes in the truth of his biography and understandably cannot have it controlled by others? It is quite easy to nitpick a biography to death.

Ellmann built up his authority not only by convincing interviewees of his probity but by earning their interest and trust in him and his work. This is why he is so aggrieved over Giedion-Welcker's letter. When an interviewee seemed to violate that attachment to the biographer and his project, Ellmann reacted as if he had been betrayed. Yet very often this kind of camaraderie between biographer and interviewee is a fleeting fiction, and both know it. Sometimes the interviewee feels abandoned—as in the case of a Rebecca West relative who was shocked that she never again heard from Victoria Glendinning after her book was published. I'm certain that Glendinning would have been surprised at this accusation of desertion, since in my experience (having followed in her tracks as a Rebecca West biographer) she has always been pleasant and agreeable to her sources. But that is the point, isn't it? The biographer's good manners are, among other things, a ploy.

Ellmann presented himself to interviewees, naturally enough, not as the biographer-hound but as one of his subject's defenders—indeed as one of the inner circle. He writes to Ethel Mannin, assuring her that he has Mrs. Yeats's backing for a biography of her husband. Mannin evidently reacted violently against one of the people he proposed to interview. But Mrs. Yeats had been apprised of everyone he expected to contact, and she had not reacted in terror or horror, Ellmann reported to Mannin. "I fully appreciate your desire to protect Yeats from unscrupulous treatment, and can only assure you again that I share it," he concluded.

Ellmann wanted his interviewees to believe he was engaging them in a cooperative enterprise. They were all a party to the biography, so to speak. But he was just as determined to remain independent. He never sought authorization for his Joyce biography—or rather, he snuck up on the idea of authorization, so that, in the end, he had the blessing of most Joyceans. But it was hard work convincing some of them to trust him. Publishers were also wary. Could this American do the job? "I wrote Macmillan," Ellmann reported to his parents in January 1953, "I couldn't meet their condition of assuring them of the Joyces' cooperation, and assumed they'd drop the idea—but they said they'd waive this condition!" Evidently Oxford University Press, which published the biography, also accepted Ellmann's terms.

Even a publishing contract, though, is hardly enough to smooth the way. "I found the man in the British foreign office who would be able to track down the Joyce material I need in their files," Ellmann updated his parents on April 5, 1953, "but he wasn't very cooperative, on the grounds that I would have to show I had the family's permission to get these papers." The biographer wasn't so sure he could obtain their cooperation.

The persistent Ellmann confronted other setbacks (his word): Joyceans who said they were writing their own reminiscences. This was discouraging, the biographer confessed to his parents. On the other hand, another Joyce friend had relinquished his plan to write a biography and had handed his papers over to Ellmann. This is what it is like for a biographer—the constant push and pull, Norman Mailer refusing me an interview because he may "someday" write about Hellman himself, the generosity of Emlyn Williams giving me a five-thousand-word piece about his memories of Hellman and his performance in her play *Montserrat*.

Ellmann's letters reveal that, like many biographers, he worked by stealth. Sometimes he felt he could not ask for interviews straightforwardly, suspecting perhaps that he would be turned down. "I have also had difficulty in arranging to meet the [Curran] sisters, though I've not broached the matter directly," he confided to his parents. This was odd, since he had already visited the Curran's house several times. "This amounts to discourtesy as well as everything else," he concluded. He had better luck with Joyce's sisters, except for Florence, who turned him down cold as she had rejected every other biographer/suitor. All Florence said was, "We were an extraordinary family and I wish to God we were what we hadn't been."

Ellmann had better luck with another source, a Mrs. Griffin, a very ebullient woman who liked to drink. Before their meetings, Ellmann would send her a note and enclose a few dollars, understanding that the poor lady could "barely afford the considerable amount of liquor she liked to take in."

Rudeness and rebuffs take their toll on a biographer. Ellmann had a hard time arranging a meeting with Joyce's sister Eva, but finally at a lunch he broke through what he called her "reserves," so that she told him a "great deal of stuff that I couldn't have got elsewhere." Suddenly energized, Ellmann began integrating her account of family history with his other material about the fortunes of the Joyces. By June 1953 the biographer was over the hump, believing he now had more material about Joyce's life than anyone except the writer's brother Stanislaus.

Still the greedy Ellmann was not satisfied, and his father felt obliged to give him a pep talk. "So what if Stanislaus is keeping some of the stuff. After all, as a brother he is entitled to some treasures after these many years of mutual struggles and battles I suppose." Could Stanislaus hold back anything that vital in the "sum total of the incidents in James Joyce's life"? Father knew best, but I can say from firsthand experience that a bloodthirsty biographer wants every last drop. Of course there is no such thing as a definitive biography, father reminded son. "So no matter how authoritative your work may be it can't be the final word."

But Ellmann was the kind of biographer who always thought he needed more sources. He treated Stanislaus gingerly, believing that a more direct approach would probably be met with resistance. But the biographer's dancing around the issues he really wanted to explore brought this query from Stanislaus, "Don't you have anything else to ask me?" Ellmann started asking, but afterward (as he admitted in "Reminiscences of a Biographer") he felt that he had really "muffed a great opportunity."

Timing is a crucial factor in the biographer's work, and Ellmann's father was right to suggest that Joyce had been dead long enough for the biographer not only to break down the resistance of interviewees but to profit from a relaxed atmosphere. "You got us quite excited today with your long story about Parisian developments, with Mrs. Jolas, Mme. Leon, Frank Budgen, etc. It's wonderful that these people are around and you are able to get their mellowed views on J. J."

One of the biographer's signal triumphs was the winning over of Harriet Shaw Weaver, one of Joyce's great benefactors. He first wrote to her on April 23, 1953, introducing himself and describing the books he had written. "It would be a great privilege to talk with you and I earnestly hope you will consent," he concluded.

Ms. Weaver was not so sure what to do, writing a few days later to her cousin, Lionel Monro, who, like her, was a Joyce literary executor. She supposed that a biography could go ahead without the estate's permission. She had never heard of Ellmann or of his books, but she decided to see Ellmann and wrote to him that he could not expect her to sit for an interview. It would all be quite informal, since she had no intention of authorizing a biography.

Ellmann disliked Weaver's abrupt tone (as he revealed in an undated letter to his parents), but he played it cool on his first visit, merely examining her signed Joyce editions and telling her that he was collecting facts and dates. He mentioned that he had to cut his visit short because his two-year-old son in Ireland was "pining for him." On one of his later letters she writes "very pleasant man."

The biographer's next move was to keep Ms. Weaver informed of his progress: an encouraging response from Joyce's brother Stanislaus and "great cooperation" from everyone. "Might I ask you about one small point?" the modest Mr. Ellmann inquires. After Ms. Weaver complies, one question leads to another, though the biographer hastens to add that Ms. Weaver need not trouble herself. He does not mean to harry her (the dog!). Now, getting the hang of it, she begins answering *at length*.

The correspondence settles into a chatty groove. They exchange news about themselves. Weaver gets to know about Ellmann's family, including an "aged poodle." Letters in 1956 keep Weaver apprised of Ellmann's progress, of whom he is seeing, and so on. By March 1958, Ellmann had a thousand-page draft he wanted Weaver to read. Was his request "too appalling?" the anxious biographer asked. Not at all, she felt honored, she replied. In the end he had her reading proofs too, and making a few corrections.

LIKE ALL SKILLFUL BIOGRAPHERS, Ellmann sought to win his sources to his side. A believer in high literary modernism, he had no qualms about presenting himself as a kind of biographer/priest, preserving the sacred Joycean and Yeatsian lore, not just the authors' texts. I do not mean that he wrote hagiography, although his method—analyses of the work, objective reporting of biographical fact—has made him largely immune to attack. He does not care to judge the author as human being (who am I to judge? is his implicit position) but is doing all he can in the service of his subject's art. As soon as Harriet Shaw Weaver recognized Richard Ellmann as one of the devout, she included him in the sanctified circle.

In effect, Ellmann elided his role as vampire in the presence of Ms. Weaver and then retired to his coffin; and in letters that do not see the light, he exulted in hounding and sucking the lifeblood from his subject. The crudity of his approach became apparent only when he wanted to publish Joyce's raunchy letters. But there, too, it was all in the service of showing how Joyce transmuted his baser elements into the gold of *Ulysses*.

To perform his sleight of hand, Ellmann wrote about biography in the traditional manner, beginning with that reference to the biographer as Judas. But he never really dealt with the negative implications of his profession—why Kipling called it a "higher form of cannibalism," or why Nabokov referred to biographers as "psycho-plagiarists," or why Henry James called them "post-mortem exploiters."

The last phrase is especially resonant to adepts in the history of biography. They will recall the unseemly rush of biographers to publish lives of Dr. Johnson. Everyone knew he was good copy, and everyone thought (at the time) that Boswell had lost out in the biographical sweepstakes because it took him seven years to publish his book, which had to take its place last in line.

Was Boswell a Judas? Dryden had already put the term in play, suggesting that the biographer was indeed a disciple gone wrong. Boswell loved to search out famous men and present himself as their acolyte. Rousseau and Johnson are the most famous targets of the Boswellian treatment. "How the devil came into your heads," wrote the outraged philosopher David Hume, "to publish in a book to all the world what you pretend I told you in private conversation." Hume is referring to a visit Boswell and two companions made to the Scottish savant, which they quickly turned into a book with the selling point that here was the unbuttoned Hume.

Certainly Boswell's contemporaries thought him shameless, and several of Johnson's friends objected to the biographer's characterizations of them. Then, as now, the literary community treated the biographer as a kind of apostate— someone who had betrayed the faith. In Boswell's case, he was the indiscreet biographer *par excellence.* He kept a journal in which he made rough with friends and foes alike and then passed it around so freely that his father—tucked away on the family estate in Scotland—got wind of his son's London capers. The idea that writers such as Paul Theroux, in his memoir of V. S. Naipaul, have cut a new path when it comes to disgraceful revelations about one of their own in the literary club simply has no merit. But then what Boswell was willing to say about intimates he also said about himself. As Adam Sisman puts it, Boswell "wanted nothing about himself to be secret." When Boswell's wife read parts of his journal, she commented that he had "emboweled himself to posterity." It is in that spirit that I write not only about other biographers but about myself.

Boswell was keenly aware of his role as Judas, and he sought every means in his biography of Johnson to suggest that both his method and his treatment of Johnson met with his subject's approval. Boswell's claims are true up to a point. Boswell revealed, for example, that Johnson had been upset about Boswell's publishing one of his letters in a travel book, *Account of Corsica*. Would it be wrong to publish Johnson's letters after his death? Boswell inquired. "Nay, Sir," Johnson replies in Boswell's biography of him, "when I am dead, you may do as you will."

Certainly Johnson understood that Boswell was recording in his journal his observations of Johnson, what Johnson said, and what others said about him. Johnson even offered (according to Boswell's journal), "I hope you shall know a great deal more of me before you write my life." But Johnson said almost the same thing to his dear friend Mrs. Thrale, who would indeed publish her biography/memoir before Boswell's.

The idea of a well-known literary figure setting up a kind of competition between biographers is not that unusual. Rebecca West in her later years received a parade of would-be biographers. Stanley Olson thought she had given him the nod and was dismayed to learn after West's death that she had left a message saying he should write a long biography and Victoria Glendinning a short one. West, a canny reviewer of biographies, seems to have shared my view: the answer to one biography is always another.

Both Johnson and West were writers who were ambivalent about biographies of themselves, even though both had spent their careers writing biography in one form or another. They knew all too well, from their own practice, how biography could invade and eviscerate. Boswell understood Johnson's wariness. He showed Johnson his journal, and the latter was highly amused by it. Boswell took that as a tacit approval of publication. But as Adam Sisman points out, Johnson never did quite authorize Boswell. In fact, Boswell was surprised to discover that Johnson said nothing about Boswell in his will. Boswell had offended enough people so that no one took it amiss when Sir John Hawkins, Johnson's literary executor, named himself as authorized biographer. After all, he had been Johnson's friend for forty years, nearly twice as long as Boswell had known Johnson.

Although Boswell would eventually surmount his doubts that Johnson meant him to be his principal biographer, like many biographers Boswell's dreams took the form of encounters that resembled a Henry James story. For example, about a year or so before completing his biography, Boswell dreamed a scene in which a very angry-looking Johnson entered his room. "My dear Sir, you certainly have nothing to say against me," Boswell cried out. "Have I nothing against you, Sir?" Johnson shouted. But what did the dream mean? Was Johnson angry because Boswell had not yet completed his biography, or upset because Boswell was writing one? It is just these kinds of dreams I have had during the writing of my seven biographies.

My most vivid ones involved Susan Sontag and Norman Mailer, both of whom, in my dreams, presented themselves in similarly equivocal fashion, never getting round to telling me in so many words what they thought of my enterprise.

Boswell had his supporters, to be sure, but he was involved in a race to produce the best biography, with Hawkins having access to certain papers that Boswell had not seen. At the time there was considerable doubt that Johnson would remain a person of interest for long. He would not have been the first literary figure famous in his time to suffer an almost immediate obscurity. Many thought Boswell would lose out by taking his time to be thorough. But in fact the competition worked to his advantage in that he was hardly alone in seeming to make hay of Johnson's demise. As one contemporary wit had it:

Boswell and Thrale, retailers of his wit,
Will tell you how he wrote, and talked, and coughed, and spit.

Mrs. Thrale, attempting to disengage herself from Boswell, claimed she had only quoted Johnson's memorable sayings with his permission, whereas Boswell had taken Johnson down at random.

Hawkins and Boswell circled each other warily, especially on the subject of Johnson's fidelity to his wife. Were there episodes of unfaithfulness that Johnson had withheld from Boswell's inspection? Did Boswell know more about the sexual side of Johnson's life than he had vouchsafed to Hawkins? In the end, both biographers studying Johnson's wayward period with Richard Savage were inclined to believe that Johnson had indulged his appetites. Adam Sisman demurs, suggesting that both biographers may have "misjudged their subject." He is right that Johnson was morally scrupulous and believed that even thoughts of sin were a kind of depravity. And Sisman is persuaded by Desmoulins's testimony that Johnson never went all the way with her. "Lust," Sisman concludes, "rather than adultery, may have been the sin for which he felt remorse."

Sisman's revisionism reminds me of Peter Ackroyd's treatment of Charles Dickens's infatuation with Ellen Ternan. Modern biographers have supposed that Dickens, unhappy in marriage, took his sexual pleasure with Ternan. But there is no real evidence to support the surmise, Ackroyd suggests. Judging by Dickens's idealization of women in his fiction and in his life, the biographer is inclined to think that the novelist did not engage in an extramarital affair.

Biography often becomes a bloodsport when biographers are competing to pursue the same subject. It is always a little startling when someone like Ackroyd calls a halt to the game. It is rather like Donald Spoto, who concluded that there was very little evidence to substantiate a significant sexual tie between Marilyn Monroe and either John or Robert Kennedy. The same stories get repeated so many times that each new biographer tends to ride the backs of others. As Sisman puts it, a propos of Hawkins and Boswell: "Each feared being scooped by the other."

Boswell won the day for several reasons. Hawkins was a dull writer, and beating Boswell to publication day ultimately meant very little. Moreover, Hawkins's view of Johnson seemed uncharitable to his first readers. He spent too much time retailing his subject's faults. Johnson's friends, some of whom had distrusted Boswell, now turned to him to rectify the authorized biography.

This too is an old story often repeated in our time. So Sonia Orwell, disliking Bernard Crick's authorized biography of her husband, turned to Michael Shelden, who published his biography after her death and was attacked by many reviewers for being too harsh on his subject. Some estates will run through several biographers before they find one tame enough to their liking. Hawkins rather reminds me of Lawrance Thompson, Robert Frost's authorized biographer, who was vilified for presenting a denigrating picture of the revered poet, which made it easier for subsequent Frost biographers to deal with his dark side.

Boswell handled the Judas issue in two contradictory yet complementary ways. First, he was aggressive. Did his critics think that because he took down Johnson's conversation he was not a "desirable member of society"? "Few, very few, need be afraid that their sayings will be recorded. Can it be imagined that I would take the trouble to gather what goes on every hedge . . . ?" Johnson, like other great men, was in a special category:

> How delighted should we have been if thus introduced into the company of Shakespeare or Dryden, of whom we know scarcely anything but their admirable writings! What pleasure would it have given us to have known their petty habits, their characteristic manners, their modes of composition and their genuine opinion of preceding writers and their contemporaries! All these are now irrevocably lost.

Boswell's genuine sadness and regret here is over death and the way it erases even the greatest of lives if care is not taken. Boswell's words are my reply to Tennyson's remark that he thanked God he knew nothing about Shakespeare. Can anyone doubt that if one of Shakespeare's letters, let alone a diary, were suddenly discovered, the world would be electrified? Boswell knew we craved what so many critics have said we should not taste.

Boswell's second line of defense was simply to play the messenger. He portrayed himself as Johnson's amanuensis—so much so that for a century after the publication of his biography, Boswell was regarded as a dope who happened to have a good memory. As Mrs. Thrale charged, all the fool could do was to render Johnson verbatim. It was a trick worthy of an idiot savant, no more.

But Boswell remains the greatest biographer—and a puppy. I'm not sure it has been sufficiently appreciated how these two sides of him go together, or how they contribute to an understanding of biography as a bloodsport. Boswell wanted to squeeze the last ounce of blood from his subject, and he bled Johnson to an unnerving extent. Yet because of his blundering naiveté, his obsession seems less calculating than ingenuous. It is as if he asks us, "What is a biographer to do?"

In *Boswell's Presumptuous Task*, Adam Sisman includes a scene that captures the essence of Boswell's method and reveals why he was simultaneously so successful and so scorned. The novelist Fanny Burney wrote a vivid account of Boswell at work, moving his chair from a table and placing it behind Johnson as he began, Sisman writes, to boom. The biographer's

> eyes goggled with eagerness; he leant his ear almost on the shoulder of the Doctor; and his mouth dropped open to catch every syllable that might be uttered; nay, he seemed not only to dread losing a word, but to be anxious not to miss a breathing. And there he remained until Johnson happened to turn and see him and shouted an ill-pleased "What do you do there, Sir? Go to the table, Sir!"

In spite of the "Sir," Johnson might as well have been speaking to his dog. Boswell was dismayed later to find in Johnson's papers certain derogatory references to him. The master did not spare his disciple the ridicule he heaped on others.

Johnson's friends, as Sisman notes, found Boswell's sycophancy funny. They joked about it all the time, portraying Boswell as a schoolboy and a teacher's pet. Boswell rarely complained of this abuse, in part because he did adore Johnson and considered him a father figure vastly superior to Boswell himself, and in part because *nothing* would be allowed to get in the way of his presumptuous task.

If there has been no biographer to equal Boswell, it is because there has been no biographer who will abase himself quite so consistently as Boswell. Biographers are often called second-raters and worse. But Boswell is the only biographer to make his role as second-rater into a work of genius. His passion for biography overrode the shame other biographers have felt in pandering to their subjects.

By the same token, Johnson deserves nearly as much credit as Boswell. However irritated he felt at this biographer who seemed to want to devour his very lifeblood, Johnson not only tolerated him but said on many occasions that he loved Boswell. Why? Read Johnson's famous essay on biography, and all is revealed. No form of literature appealed to Johnson more than biography, and here was Boswell not only just as deeply committed to biography but also determined to make Johnson the greatest biographical subject in the history of the world.

Sisman shrewdly suggests that Johnson watching Boswell watch him became more and more the Johnson of Boswell's dreams. In Boswell's presence, in other words, Johnson learned to act more and more like the Johnson Boswell craved. This is likely, since after Johnson's death, Boswell found evidence of a master who in his interactions with others was less dignified and less principled. Johnson realized, in other words, that he was serving as Boswell's model. In those moments when Johnson treats Boswell roughly, he is, it would seem, chafing against the role his biographer has assigned him.

Yet these two men, whatever their differences, formed a team, a kind of walking Platonic dialogue about life, literature, politics, religion, philosophy, and much else. It is the friction and the constant lubrication of their relationship that make their relationship so sporting. It is no wonder that writers from Conan Doyle to Rex Stout and many others have found this idea of a male duo so attractive. Boswell made of biography a game of detection and a sport. Both his papers and his testimony in the biography show that his quest for biographical data was bloodthirsty. He raced all over London, wrote numerous letters, pestered whomever he could contact to supply him with material about Johnson. No biographer before Boswell—certainly not Johnson—had ever regarded biography as a genre to be pursued with such diligence. Boswell checked and rechecked his sources, and threw out many anecdotes he could not verify even when they made for tasty reading. He was indiscriminate only in the sense that at the collection stage no item was too trivial, no word about Johnson too insignificant, to drop into the mill of biographical research.

Boswell is the dog with his nose to the ground, sniffing for clues everywhere. He is not embarrassed to sit behind his master at table. What decent man would do a thing like that? Only a biographer—no gentleman indeed! For his time, Boswell could not have been more transgressive. Even those who read his biography and enjoyed it heartily went on to deplore his methods and revelations, just as critics and readers still do in those reviews and letters that make the biographer out to be a McCarthyite: "Have you no shame, biographer? Have you no shame at last?"

Since the discovery of Boswell's papers in this century, the view of the biographer as the dunce stenographer—no more than the inquisitive schoolboy—has been shattered. Boswell worked up his notes, his journal, and all the materials he collected and collated into dramatic scenes that everywhere demonstrate the work of a master artist. It is Johnson before us, but Johnson shaped into Boswellian attire. He is more august, more steady, more magnificent than later biographers have presented. As Adam Sisman points out, Boswell was in search of a hero, a father figure, and a man who was everything that the unsteady Boswell could not be. In Sisman's memorable phrase, Boswell emphasized the "effort of collection, rather than the art of composition."

This presentation of himself as a human tape recorder had other consequences as well. It disguised not only the fact that Boswell was writing, in essence, a memoir, but that as a consequence he had every right to publish what Johnson said. So many of his subject's words were directed to Boswell himself. It is his own experience that Boswell is recounting, even when it is not a scene involving him and Johnson. The very process of collecting, collating, and interpreting makes someone else's life a part of the biographer's existence. What right has anyone to say he cannot render his own experience, which, of course, impinges on others? And this is so for all biographers, even if they did not know their subjects. They are synthesizing the testimony of dozens and sometimes hundreds of interviews and memoirs and documents and making these materials into a new creation, part of the substance of the world.

The biographer is one of the many who have projected themselves onto the biographical subject's life. Indeed, every time someone comments on our behavior, our sense of ourselves is violated. People publish each other to the world every day. And those who publish in print can expect to be published about in turn. All this Boswell knew, and he could never understand why what people said—if what they said had special interest—should not be memorialized in print.

When Boswell's interviewees asked to read the proofs of his biography in order to see how their contributions had been used, Boswell sometimes accepted, sometimes rejected, and sometime ignored their requests. It all had to do, in his mind, with their motivations. He knew, as all seasoned biographers do, that some interviewees will want to renege on what they said or, in this case, try to erase what Johnson had said about them, especially if (as was likely) the great man's words had not been complimentary. If Boswell had simply passed around his biography to everyone who had contributed to it, he might have been nitpicked to death, ending up with, as Sisman rightly observes, a bland book.

In cases where Boswell's friends asked for permission to read proof, he usually consented because there was every chance they might improve on what they had said or add more details. Certainly this has been my experience as a biographer. When Diana Trilling asked to see my biography of Lillian Hellman before publication and made it a stipulation in our interview, I agreed. The result is that she considerably improved not only her wording but also my own without removing any remark I wished to print.

On the other hand, I confess I reneged on an offer to show William Styron the part of my Norman Mailer biography in which Styron figures. I had interviewed Styron, who told me a strange and riveting story of an incident in which a New York editor had stabbed his wife. This event had occurred some seven or eight years before Norman Mailer stabbed his second wife. Styron remembered that Mailer, who also knew the editor, had said at the time that he wished he had the guts to do something like that. Styron recounted the whole story almost in a stage whisper. Part of it was not new because in truncated form it had also appeared in Hilary Mills's Mailer biography. But Styron gave me much more detail—or rather, I suspect that Mills, a friend of Styron's, chose not to tell the whole story—perhaps at Styron's request.

I wondered about Styron's motivations in telling me the story. He and Mailer had feuded for years but recently had patched things up and were on very good terms. In fact, Styron presented his willingness to speak with me as part of his effort to reconcile with Mailer. I thought it an odd way to do so, but like a good biographer I held my tongue. Styron spoke in such a low, dramatic voice that I worried his words would not be audible on my tape recording. But he also spoke so distinctly and deliberately that afterward I found the recording to be very clear.

After our interview, Styron had second thoughts. He had offered to give me entrée into his archive at Duke University. I'd find some correspondence with Mailer there, he told me. When I called him to inquire about the letter he was supposed to address to the archivist on my behalf, he coldly said he had changed his mind. "But I've bought a nonrefundable plane ticket on the strength of your offer," I said. "That's your problem," he said, and hung up.

When the *New York Post* published an interview with me and retold part of the stabbing story, Styron and Mailer ganged up on me, suggesting I had sensationalized the event. Like a good Boswell, though, I had it all recorded and had reproduced in my biography virtually a transcript of what Styron said. None of this would have surprised or shocked Boswell in the least.

I don't blame Styron for his ambivalence, though I do think his unwillingness to take responsibility for the interview cowardly. A few years earlier I had contacted him about an interview for my Lillian Hellman biography. He wrote me a card that he regretted he could not see me because he had promised her to speak only to her authorized biographer. I wondered if perhaps his speaking with me about Mailer was an attempt to make amends for that earlier rebuff.

I say amends because Richard Wilbur, who did consent to an interview about Hellman, told me that Hellman had virtually ordered several of her friends to speak only to her authorized biographer. Wilbur resented this command and seemed to suggest there were others who did as well. Certainly I had no trouble finding enough people to speak with me about Hellman. It was Wilbur who first pointed out to me that Hellman's instruction meant that she was asking him to keep silent about his own experience—or rather, dictating whom he could talk to. I have often wondered why more friends of the famous do not see it Wilbur's way. Styron, whose rebuff was quite polite and with a hint of regret, may have thought what Wilbur expressed aloud. I also received more than one long agonizing letter from the late John Hersey, another Hellman friend having trouble with Hellman's fiat. I kept writing to him because I thought at some point he would break his oath. He never did, but I could see that as a journalist who did his own share of investigative reporting, he found his promise to Hellman burdensome, perhaps even questionable. How can you be your own person when someone else is dictating the terms of your engagement with the world?

Boswell never relented in asserting his right to publish private conversations. Even though his biography was acclaimed almost immediately as a classic, and even though it sold well, the biographer became a kind of pariah. He could still be found at his club, and he still was invited to parties, but his friends confided to him that they could not always admit him to their company. Certain objections had been raised as to the propriety of admitting a man to polite society who might very well publish a report of his social engagements.

Boswell scoffed at those who feared he would expose their conversations, rightly pointing out that most conversations did not deserve to be repeated. Johnson's were the exception, not the rule. But there is no question that Boswell's more important friends like Edmund Burke curbed their quips in his presence. He was simply not a reliable confidant. And, of course, they were right. Boswell's mission was to reveal; theirs to conceal.

I know only too well what Boswell felt. While writing the biography of Jill Craigie, I carried a small tape recorder around with me. Like Boswell, I accompanied her husband Michael Foot on various jaunts to his home ground in Plymouth, to his holiday sojourn in Dubrovnik, and to the restaurants, parties, and receptions he attended in London. If Boswell spent something like four hundred days in Johnson's company over a twenty-one-year period, I was at Foot's side for approximately a hundred days over a three-year period. I have hundreds of hours of him talking and of others talking to him.

Better than Boswell who saw Johnson mainly on social occasions, I lived with Foot about ten days at a time, not merely sleeping in his library but with his permission examining every book and drawer in his large house in Hampstead. He had no files but rather had strewn his archive all over his domicile. Some treasures were to be found between the covers of his annotated books. This unprecedented access—the long conversations over meals, and the tape recorder running all the while Foot reminisced about his wife, his political career, his family, and everything else under the sun—is surely a remarkable gift to any biographer.

But that gift had consequences. One of Foot's closest associates, a woman who promised Jill she would look after Michael, regarded me with a suspicious eye from day one of my entrance into Foot's home. While Foot had no qualms—he had contributed to and admired extravagantly my biography of Rebecca West (one of Jill's heroes)—this guardian of Jill's wishes would always make some pointed remark about my little black box silently recording every remark, no matter how offhand or revealing. She was a Labour party hack whose job it was to shepherd Foot about and to try to check his generous, ebullient, and forthcoming nature.

I could see that she was aghast at the liberty I had been given and then appalled as I delved into certain family secrets that I told Michael early on I could not suppress because I felt they were at the heart of his relationship with Jill. As a biographer himself, he agreed with me—even telling me about his regrets in deciding to suppress the story about Aneurin Bevan and his early love. Michael despised authorized biographies and understood that I felt similarly. In fact, I told him in some detail about the efforts of Susan Sontag and Martha Gellhorn to suppress my biographies of them. Then he read my revised biography of Gellhorn and published a glowing review of it.

The trouble started when certain family members objected to the draft of the biography I sent them. Michael, on the other hand, while calling for some revisions, generally gave the book a bravo. But then the party hack, the family & co., started to work on him. Sensitive to his family's feelings, he began to renege on our agreement, calling for all sorts of revisions—indeed demanding them in direct refutation of our understanding, which, by the way, I had recorded.

As of this writing, the book is about to be published, and I have resisted most of the calls to suppress material. Whether there will be further acrimony or not, I cannot say, but I already have it in mind to write a piece called "Becoming Jill Craigie's Deauthorized Biographer."

Boswell was just such an outlaw, even though Johnson had called him—coining the word—the most "clubbable" of men. My relationship with Foot was just as warm and jolly. Although I did not regard him as a father figure, as Boswell did Johnson, the difference in our ages (Foot is now ninety-two and I am fifty-seven) made for a similar kind of teacher-pupil relationship, though I hasten to add that Foot never treated me with the asperity and condescension that Johnson heaped on Boswell. That side of Foot emerged only after his family persuaded him that I had betrayed confidences. Then I began to get letters that sounded very Johnsonian indeed—"Don't talk such nonsense!" or some such phrase would checker Foot's responses to my accusations that he was censoring my biography.

Imagine that Johnson had lived to read Boswell's life of him. Do you really think that Johnson would not have hammered the man who he once joked was a "spy upon me." The joshing Johnson would have given way to the censorious doctor.

Boswell was a much more sociable and sensitive man than I am. He minded being ostracized. But then I have had the benefit of reading Boswell and of absorbing the history of biographers who have ended as hunted men, so to speak, the sport of critics who ridicule and ride their hobbyhorses against the genre I have staked my heart to. By nature a solitary, I regard the isolation of biographers like me with equanimity, recognizing that I am fair game. I have never been commissioned to do a biography and have always been my own man, so I can hardly resent the fact that others find my invasions of their lives despicable.

The harsher critics consider biographers parasites. To Boswell this would hardly have been a knock. Would any present-day biographer place the following notice in the *Public Advertiser*? "Boswell has so many invitations in consequence of his *Life of Johnson* that he may be *literally* said to *live* upon his deceased friend." The biographer was fond of puffing his own work under other names or in anonymous announcements. He disregarded those who regarded his enterprise with distaste. As Adam Sisman reports, Edmund Burke, discussing Johnson's biographers, exclaimed to the bluestocking Hannah More: "How many maggots have crawled out of that great body."

To be sure, Boswell's methods were appreciated by certain of his contemporaries, just as modern biography has its proponents among a few, a very few critics. One of Boswell's correspondents, William Elford, later a Member of Parliament and a Fellow of the Royal Society, wrote to him: "This kind of biography appears to me perfectly new. Instead of describing your characters, you exhibit them to the reader. He finds himself in their company, and becomes an auditor of the conversations, which have all the dignity of the best moral writings, soften'd by the ease, the wit, and the familiarity of colloquial manners." But that was the rub: for every reader who enjoyed the biography, there was another who deplored the biographer's familiarity with his subject. For Boswell the biographer had indeed made an exhibition of himself, of his subject, and of his subject's companions, and to make an exhibition—then, as now—is to imply an unseemly show, a flaunting of what should be private, secret, and discreet. To make the reader an "auditor" is thrilling but also disturbing, like picking up the phone and listening in on a mate's conversation or reading another's mail. The familiarity of Boswell's approach seemed excessive to many of his contemporaries—and I daresay to this age when it reads one day my memoir/biography of Michael Foot.

Boswell could never understand why the best society shunned him, why he could not obtain a seat in Parliament, why he did not succeed as a lawyer or in attaining the various public offices to which he aspired. After all, he had given so many people so much pleasure, not only as Johnson's biographer but also as an engaging human being. He was, quite simply, fun. I've never come across a reference to Boswell as tedious, though I suppose in his melancholy mood he might have been so. Rather, his friends always tried to lift him out of his depression because they longed to enjoy the ebullient Boswell.

After completing his life of Johnson, Boswell drifted. He was never able to reassert the discipline he had shown in composing Johnson's biography. He compared his fate to his contemporaries—those men who had succeeded at the bench and in politics—and he lamented that they "held a creditable and actual situation in society, whereas I held none."

Adam Sisman concludes his stirring book on Boswell's presumptuous task by lauding the *Life of Johnson* as a "pioneering work which opened up new possibilities for biography." But "it was also unique: never again will there be such a combination of a subject, author, and opportunity." Perhaps so. But I plan to test this judgment in my life of Foot.

WHAT HAPPENED TO BIOGRAPHY after Boswell? A. O. J. Cockshut provides an eloquent explanation in *Truth to Life: The Art of Biography in the Nineteenth Century*. The biographical subject became sacrosanct; that is, anyone thought deserving of a biography became almost a new category of being. In Johnson's *Life of Savage*, the subject had been judged simply as a person like any other: "Johnson assumes, admirably and rightly as it seems to me," Cockshut argues, "that since one is a man before one is any particular kind of man, so moral principles apply to one's basic human status, not to one's function in society, or one's natural bent." In other words, that Savage was a poet gave him no special status in the biographer's eyes.

The Romantics changed this universalizing Enlightenment view and elevated the poet into a revered realm that Modernists (as I will argue later) reified. Thus Cockshut quotes Shelley's ringing phrase that poets are the "unacknowledged legislators of the world." This conceit implies, Cockshut notes, that a poet "cannot quite be judged by ordinary standards."

The dreadful consequences of this poet worship are evident when Norman Mailer, for example, defended the late Jack Henry Abbott, a murderer, because he was also a sensitive writer who taught Mailer much about life in prison. One of my harsher chapters on Mailer deals with the Abbott controversy. To be sure, Mailer did not excuse Abbott's crime, but he certainly contended that Abbott deserved special consideration because of his powerful writing. When I wrote my Mailer biography, I did not quite understand this episode's significance. I realize now that in part I was responding to a romanticism gone decadent, a romanticism without moral compass, a romanticism besotted with the cult of the writer.

But it is not just writers who deserve a niche in heaven—or a pedestal in Westminster Abbey—but also the Carlylean Great Man of history (an offshoot of romanticism) who is also deserving of consecration. As Cockshut observes of Carlyle's biography of Cromwell: "He assumes that Cromwell, because he was a genius, was in some special, intimate way in tune with the harmonies of the whole universe and that, for this reason, he was not to be judged by ordinary moral standards."

Carlyle's narrative exhibits Cromwell's uniqueness rather than arguing for it. Cockshut analyzes this "unexceptionable" yet telling description of Cromwell in his native fen country:

> Here of a certainty Oliver did walk and look about him habitually, during those five years from 1631 to 1636; a man studious of many temporal and many eternal things. His cattle grazed, his ploughs tilled the earth, the heavenly skies and infernal abysses overarched and underarched him here.

This is a man in tune with the creator and creation; a man who lives his theology. Read in the context of Carlyle's three-volume biography, the "plain implication is that a neighbouring royalist squire was not so overarched and underarched. The sky itself is credited with a party preference," Cockshut concludes.

It was not always so with Carlyle, Cockshut reminds us. A few years earlier he had written "The Sanspotato is the selfsame stuff as the superfinest Lord Lieutenant." Carlyle forgot himself, Cockshut suggests. Romanticism, I would say, had got hold of the biographer.

But if Carlyle turned increasingly Romantic, he was not yet a modernist, the critic who declares we must separate the life from the work, the work from the life, and never the twain can be synthesized. Carlyle would have found such views preposterous. Once again, Cockshut identifies the kind of synthesis that modernism rejects, thus draining the blood out of biography. Cockshut quotes Carlyle's portrait of Coleridge in his biography of John Sterling:

> [I]n walking he shuffled rather than decisively stept; and a lady once remarked, he could never fix which side of the garden-walk would suit him best, but continually shifted, in corkscrew fashion, and kept trying both.

How Johnson and Boswell would have applauded this passage, welcoming its humor and what Cockshut calls Carlyle's "tongue-in-cheek tribute to the sage and philosopher." If Coleridge was a genius, he was a genius at trying to straddle two positions at once, inevitably contorting himself so that he could never take a firm step in either direction. Here Coleridge's wayward walk becomes the corporeal equivalent of his meandering prose.

Cockshut supplies a few more significant examples of the way Carlyle fuses the man to his work, but suffice it to say that the biographer, in Cockshut's words, has neatly performed a "hatchet-job." In this respect, Carlyle was a nineteenth-century Boswell, who decried the complacency and euphemistic style of his fellow biographers. The effort to lionize literary figures like Coleridge troubled Carlyle, even as he failed to see how he had idolized Cromwell.

The urge not to be a Boswell was powerful among nineteenth-century biographers, for, as Cockshut notes, "The moral superiority of the nineteenth century to the eighteenth century was a fixed idea to which writers of all schools could appeal." That superiority found its expression in Thackeray's attack on Swift's coarseness, and in the sentiments of biographers such as John Gibson Lockhart, Sir Walter Scott's nephew and his authorized biographer, who pointedly steered clear of Boswellian biography, refusing to render the kind of table talk that makes Boswell such delicious reading. Other nineteenth-century titans such as Thomas Babington Macaulay praised Boswell's genius in one breath and deplored his vulgarity in the other. Indeed, nineteenth-century editors bowdlerized Boswell, publishing anthologies that featured Johnson's sayings and avoided the biographer's scenic revelations of human character.

SINCE THE PUBLICATION of Boswell's work, the notion of the biographer as Judas has intensified. When James Anthony Froude published his biography of Carlyle, the accusations of betrayal may well have led Oscar Wilde to make his famous quip about the biographer as Judas—though Wilde had other examples to pick from in the political realm: Trevelyan's life of Macaulay, in which the subject appears as pathetic, or Morley's life of Gladstone, in which the great statesman is shown to be "totally mistaken on religious questions," as Cockshut puts it.

Froude, at any rate, initiates the modern phase of biography as bloodsport. In every sense of the word he was Carlyle's follower. Both Froude's slavishness and independence contributed to what Ian Hamilton in *Keepers of the Flame* calls the "most heartfelt and compelling of Victorian biographies." For the purposes of this book, though, this is not saying enough. I am inclined to favor, rather, Cockshut's startling conclusion— Boswell notwithstanding—that Froude is the "greatest of all our biographers." Froude is so because he broke the civil code by which biographers had lived since Boswell.

On the subject of biography, Froude took Carlyle at his word:

> How delicate, decent is English biography, bless its mealy mouth! A Damocles' sword of *Respectability* hangs forever over the poor English life-writer (as it does over poor English life in general), and reduces him to the verge of paralysis. . . . The English biographer has long felt that if in writing his biography he wrote down anything that could possibly offend any other man, he had written wrong. The plain consequence was that, properly speaking, no biography whatever could be produced.

Carlyle, a big exaggerator, was not exaggerating here. While working on a second edition of his life of Johnson, Boswell received more than one letter asking him to make sure that he excised from his book any words that might offend the living or the dead!

By Carlyle's time this dread of hurting anyone's feelings had only grown worse, and would continue well into the twentieth century. A character in *The Forsyte Saga* remarks ironically that he is grateful for English reticence. Of course his remark is tongue in cheek, since at that very moment the Forsytes are gossiping about how one of their own has left his wife for his family's German governess. Reticence applied, in other words, only to printed publication.

When it came to his own biography, Carlyle was not nearly so brutal minded. In his 1873 will, he stated, "I had really rather that there should be none." He thought he had published enough autobiographical work to make his life plain—a curious comment by a man who devoted decades to writing biographies. Then almost immediately he changed his mind, realizing that biographers would surely write about him, whatever his wishes. So would the trusted Froude take on the job?

Carlyle gave his man a box of papers, including letters, diaries, memoirs, and much other personal matter, "to burn freely as I might think right," Froude later recounted in *My Relations with Carlyle*, a biographer's apologia published a decade or so after Froude's death.

Disciples, I suppose, do not think it fit to catch their masters in contradictions. At any rate, Froude did not seem disturbed that the same man who exhorted him "to keep back nothing and to extenuate nothing" could so easily consign his papers to the flames. Froude declared his independence from Carlyle with regard to one point: "I was left free to deal with the story as I might think right, and that I was not to be interfered with." Of course this in itself is a very Carlylean attitude.

If Cockshut believes that Froude surpasses Boswell, it is in part because Carlyle—in spite of his contradictory statements—made it possible for his biographer to have access to even his most private affairs. Unlike Johnson, Carlyle burned nothing, even if he contemplated conflagration. Even better, Carlyle made no excuses for himself, relieving his biographer from having to work through his subject's defenses. As a biographer, Froude was freed from the biographer's shame that he is exposing his subject—not that Carlyle's friends, family, or readers would see it that way.

The trouble started when Jane Welsh Carlyle died. It had been a contentious marriage, though how contentious the husband did not appreciate until he began to collect Jane's letters. Thunderstruck is not too vehement a word to describe how aghast he was at his egotism and the toll it took on his wife's humor and health. His eloquent wife's letters could leave him in no doubt that he had behaved like a domestic tyrant. She had sacrificed herself for this demanding, irascible, and ungrateful husband. Carlyle read her indictment and immediately pleaded guilty. He could now see what a brute he had been, and to expiate his sins wrote a memoir that seconded Jane's letters of complaint even as he lauded her virtues. How such an intelligent woman and wonderful writer had put up with him he could not imagine. He was, in short, undeserving of her love.

This kind of male reaction is not that rare, actually. H. G. Wells reacted much the same way when his Jane died. He published her stories and wrote about his own unworthiness to be her husband. I found much the same kind of grief-and-guilt in Michael Foot's response to his wife's death. Calling on him just two months after the grand public memorial he had orchestrated for Jill, I found him white as a sheet, a ghost of himself, really, as he kept repeating, "She was the best of us all." Wells, however, was the only one of the three men to actually publish his remorse. Carlyle annotated and wrote up his response to Jane's letters, but the decision to publish he left to Froude.

Like Carlyle, Foot wanted his Jill's story told. Unlike Carlyle, Foot has lived to see it told, which makes me in the annals of biography as a bloodsport a less fortunate biographer than Froude. On the other hand, Froude had to bear only the weight of what he supposed Carlyle wanted from him as a biographer. That is, unlike Foot, Carlyle was not around to contradict himself or engage in a contest with his biographer. If Carlyle had been alive to read Froude's biography of him, he might have realized that he wanted the truth told only *up to a point.*

Thus Froude found himself in a situation that no biographer before him had ever confronted—complete access to his subject's most intimate papers and a free hand. Boswell had to tussle with Sir John Hawkins and others to retrieve Johnson's letters and manuscripts, and there were stories he suspected that Johnson would not want told. Even Boswell, hardly a model of discretion, could not brook the furor that would have been aroused if he had, for example, written up the scene in which Johnson dallied with a woman younger than his wife, who had rejected Samuel's advances. It would have been a juicy scene, since Johnson's fondling had occurred while his wife slept in an adjoining room.

Carlyle was no adulterer, though he had carried on a silly flirtation with a noblewoman, a foolish affair that pained and embarrassed Jane in much the same way Jill Craigie found Michael Foot's similar infatuation with a lady of fashion humiliating. These men thought only of themselves, and this is what the candid Carlylean biographer has to show—though he then hazards the opprobrium heaped on him by the great man's acolytes.

But what a dilemma for Froude! Thomas Carlyle, the great-man theorist of the Great Man Theory of History, would have to be shown at home as a little man. As Ian Hamilton puts it in *Keepers of the Flame*, the biographer "knew more than he wanted to know." Froude did consider whitewashing the story of Carlyle's bedeviled marriage, but what kind of Carlylean could he call himself then?

But Froude was thinking not just as a biographer but also as a disciple. He was afraid that if he did not write the biography, his hero would be at the mercy of a malicious posterity. Certainly Froude was correct in believing that Carlyle would have his detractors. But it seems never to have occurred to him that later biographers with no investment in Victorian values might have been more sympathetic than Carlyle's contemporaries, since they would not be part of the cultural arena in which Carlyle was so dominant a figure. Of course one age can hardly anticipate another, but at the very least there was the possibility that with passions cooled, later biographers would not be quick to judge Carlyle but to understand him.

Still, as a Carlylean biographer myself, I empathize with Froude. He has a story to tell, and he believes he can tell it better than anyone else. And yet he dreads the consequences. In my own biography, I believe I have been true to Jill, but some of Michael's friends, who have already issued fair warning, have slated me for attack. The person to protect, in both cases, is the man, the public figure whose reputation counts for far more than his wife's—even among the wife's friends (with a few notable exceptions).

What makes Froude in my book the greatest English biographer is the full weight he gave to Jane's testimony. How could he do otherwise, you might say, since Carlyle himself had accepted the justness of her verdict? Yet it remains true that in being faithful to her, and to Carlyle, Froude forever changed the nature of biography. In other words, Froude, not Lytton Strachey, who is so often acclaimed as destroying the proprieties of Victorian biography, is the true revolutionary.

Froude never said so, but I suspect he believed that while Carlyle was a great man, Jane was the greater human being. She recognized and applauded her husband's greatness, but her understanding of their marriage and of their world was, as Carlyle appreciated when he read her letters, far greater than his own. I had the good fortune to ask my Carlyle, Michael Foot, what Jill had taught him: "Everything," he exulted. He freely conceded that he had married a woman with a greater imagination than his own. Foot's latest biographer, a British academic specializing in political biographies, will most likely miss this aspect of the marriage, even though he knew Jill. The only information about Jill he seemed to want from me was a statement as to whether I thought Jill had affected Michael's stance on public policy. Michael would say yes, but Jill herself, rather like Jane, thought her husband rather obtuse when he came to her concerns. When I turned up considerable evidence of Foot's meanness about money and the running of the household—evidence found in Jill's letters and in her daughter's reminiscences—Michael would not have it. He did not say so, but I could tell he could not abide this example of his littleness.

Both Carlyle and Foot realized, in retrospect, just how much their wives had enlarged their worlds. This is what Froude sought to show even as he exposed the disturbing details of a troubled marriage. Michael Foot, just as egotistical as Carlyle, did not exhibit Carlyle's roughness, but there is a parallel to be drawn. In a cabinet in Michael's bedroom I found a thank-you note written after a party in the Foot home. The guest had compared Michael and Jill to the Carlyles. Did the writer realize the remark was a provocation as much as a compliment?

In Froude's conscientious hands, biography becomes a provocation but also a tragic human drama that is the equal of a great novel. Cockshut captures the central dynamic of Froude's achievement: "Froude's whole assessment of his subject's character required the idea that he was strong in great things and weak in little, that his far-ranging vision and majestic genius made him impossible on the cramped domestic stage." What is more, Jane, like Jill Craigie, understood this dynamic. Even if both women deplored their husbands' domestic deficiencies (neither man had the slightest idea of how to help make a home), they shared and reinforced their husband's quest for greatness. These men were heroes in their own homes—even as Jane and Jill complained that their great men should have more of a capacity to understand the woman's point of view.

Froude was no feminist in theory, but in practice he was nothing less. Cockshut fastens on just the passage that demonstrates why Froude is the superior biographer:

> Miss Welsh, it is probable, would have passed through life more pleasantly had she married someone in her own rank of life; Carlyle might have gone through it successfully with his mother or sister to look after him. But, after all is said, trials and sufferings are only to be regretted when they have proved too severe to be borne. Though the lives of the Carlyles were not happy, yet if we look at them from the beginning to the end they were grandly beautiful. Neither of them probably under other conditions would have risen as high as in fact they achieved; and the main question is not how happy men and women have been in this world, but what they have made of themselves. I well remember the bright assenting laugh with which she once responded to some words of mine when the propriety was being discussed of relaxing the marriage laws. I had said that the true way to look at marriage was a discipline of character.

Whether or not Froude is right about "the true way"—an American in pursuit of happiness might bridle at the biographer's Victorian earnestness—it is Jane's "bright assenting laugh" that drives the point home.

If Froude erred, it was in taking too seriously *all* of Jane's complaints just because she expressed them. Some people are complainers, you know? Letters can distort as well as reveal. Carlyle himself, a devotee of the nineteenth-century biographer's belief in documents and in printed evidence, may have himself taken his wife's letters a touch too seriously as evidence of her true self, the self that never complained as loudly in person as at her writing table. At any rate, this is how Michael

Foot reacted, when he rightly pointed out how congenial his marriage to Jill had been, the evidence of which is not always found in Jill's letters but is readily apparent in interviews with her friends.

Cockshut does a superb job of showing how much humor there is in Jane's letters and how the "mixture of callousness, comedy and violence is very Carlylean. . . . It is noticeable too how many shared jokes there are in letters, and how many of these depend upon traditions in Carlyle's own family before they were married." The same could be said for Jill, who embraced the large Foot family and found her affection reciprocated.

As Cockshut reiterates in his penetrating study of nineteenth-century biography, it is all a matter of equilibrium. Biographers get into trouble when readers become upset by what they regard as imbalance. Writing so much about the Carlyles' stormy household upset Froude's Victorian readers, those precursors of the Joyce Carol Oates school of anti-pathography.

No sooner did Froude publish his authorized biography than Carlyle's niece, Mary, abetted by a host of Carlyle's friends and scholars, attacked it. The anti-Froudian position—as Ian Hamilton aptly sums it up in *Keepers of the Flame*—held that the "great and splendid prophet had found himself shackled to a neurotic malcontent whose gifts and virtues he had, with characteristic magnanimity, exaggerated and then, after death, impetuously glorified. There *were* no faults to be fastened on, unless great generosity of spirit should be deemed a fault."

The Carlyle family even employed a distinguished American scholar, Charles Eliot Norton, to attack Froude. Norton, a friend of Carlyle's, had always disliked Froude, calling him "an accomplished flatterer" who plied his profession as biographer with "cynical insincerity." Norton mined the Carlyle papers in an effort to overturn Froude, whose other books had shown him to be sloppy when it came to transcribing texts. Norton easily found errors, the kind of typos and botched transcriptions that small-minded reviewers enjoy pouncing on. Norton even resorted to the traditional reviewer's ploy: If he had found *these* errors, God knows how many more the biographer had committed! Froude, in short, was a fraud.

Froude did make significant mistakes, but posterity has cleared him of mendacity. His view of the Carlyles remains persuasive, however many shadings subsequent biographers such as Phyllis Rose in *Parallel Lives* put on the story. Froude penned his defense, *My Relations with Carlyle*, for posthumous publication. Nothing he could have done in his lifetime, not even publishing his defense, would have altered the terms of what had become a bloodsport, in which Froude was called "a Mephistopheles" and a "continental liar."

These two epithets are revealing: the first suggests the biographer is a devil who insinuates himself into the subject's life; the second implies that what Froude did was un-English. Of course it was. It would have been all right to gossip about a troubled marriage but certainly not to publish it to the world.

The truth is that Carlyle's followers and friends could not bear to confess their anger over his shortcomings and could not admit how humiliated they felt by Froude's revelations. Froude understood that he, the messenger, was attacked because of the need to preserve the biographical subject as sacrosanct. Richard Aldington would later have to learn the same lesson when he took on another great national hero, T. E. Lawrence.

Froude realized that anything he could say would be regarded as self-serving. So he asked Sir James Stephen, a co-executor along with Froude of the Carlyle literary estate, to conduct a thorough examination of the case against him. Stephen, a High Court judge, the brother of the esteemed biographer Leslie Stephen (Virginia Woolf's father), issued an exoneration of Froude distributed privately in a pamphlet. Later Froude quoted Stephen in *My Relations with Carlyle*:

> Of him [Carlyle] I will make only one remark in justice to you [Froude]. He did not use you well. He threw upon you the responsibility of a decision which he ought to have taken himself in a plain, unmistakable way. He considered himself bound to expiate the wrongs which he had done his wife. If he had done this himself it would have been a courageous thing; but he did not do it himself. He did not even decide for himself that it should be done after his death. If any courage was shown in the matter, it was shown by you, and not by him. You took the responsibility of deciding for him that it ought to be done. You took the odium of doing it, of avowing to the world the faults and weaknesses of one whom you regarded as your teacher and master. In order to present to the world a true picture of him as he really was, you, well knowing what you were about, stepped into a pillory in which you were charged with treachery, violation of confidence, and every imaginable base motive, when you were in fact guilty of no other fault than that of practicing Mr Carlyle's great doctrine that men ought to tell the truth.

If Froude is culpable, it is because he did not quite tell the whole truth. He shrank from telling the one secret that would have made his biography an even greater work of art. He was like a novelist (Froude had written fiction) who cannot bring himself to work into his narrative one of the mainsprings of his character's motivations. He understood the damage he had done to his own masterpiece, however, because he revealed that secret in *My Relations with Carlyle*, which has become, in a sense, what the *Compson Appendix* is to *The Sound and the Fury*—a retrospective commentary on a great story that puts that story into a larger historical context.

What Froude did not tell in his biography reveals what Ian Hamilton calls his "bewildered consciousness." Froude wrote as if his biography told enough of the truth. This is the "blemish in this great biography," Cockshut observes. "The blemish is not the reticence itself, but the prevarication involved in pretending that reticence has not been required."

Froude hints in the biography at what he leaves out. Why is he so emphatic, for example, that Carlyle would not have married if Jane had not accepted him? Why does Froude say it would have been all right—if not the best possible outcome—for Carlyle's mother and sister to have looked after him? Why did husband and wife have separate bedrooms? Why did Jane's letters evoke such an agony of violence, anger, and frustration, each partner seeming to be searching from some kind of outlet denied to them? Observing the marriage over many years, Froude might well have wondered about the cause of its trouble.

Then one of Jane's confidants confided to Froude what had been the matter. Jane said her husband was impotent; the marriage, it seems, had not been consummated. Although he had only one source, Froude had no reason to doubt it, any more than I can doubt what Jill Craigie's housekeeper told me about Jill's marriage. In both cases the source is a woman devoted to the friend she is describing, a woman who deeply feels the pain of her friend's admission to her, a woman whose remarks on other matters not only fit the pattern of the biographical subject's life but can also be corroborated by others.

Like Cockshut, I find it hard to be hard on Froude for his prevarication. In *My Relations with Carlyle* he explains that the impotence was "something which I would infinitely rather have remained in ignorance of, because I could not forget it, because it must necessarily influence me in all that I might say, while I considered I must endeavour if possible to conceal." As I type these words I have in mind a letter from the late Paul Foot, sent to me after he read a draft of *To Be a Woman: The Life of Jill Craigie*. The letter praises my book but deplores my decision to include a chapter about the one period in the Foot marriage that nearly caused it to founder. To Paul I am merely sensationalizing a life that reads very well without my account of Michael's infidelity. To me, on the other hand, this fraught period in Jill's life speaks to her essence as a person, to her view of Michael, and is necessary, if for no other reason, because it explains why as the couple grew older their marriage actually strengthened and was at its happiest. Paul & Co. find the chapter demeaning—a poor repayment for Michael's hospitality to me, his openness and trust.

The biographer as betrayer: it is the perennial charge, leveled at the disciple but also at the professional biographer, the one who goes about looking for juicy subjects.

14

WHAT WOULD HAPPEN if Thomas Carlyle returned to write biography in the twentieth century? He did—though he called himself Richard Aldington: "And the principle that you are not to say anything impolite about the work or character of a writer who has been dead 20 years destroys both honest criticism and honest biography. Why must we be so damned mealy-mouthed?" Aldington wrote on August 15, 1952, to Alan Bird, who was helping him to research a life of T. E. Lawrence (TEL).

Aldington, a survivor of the trenches in World War I, a poet who edited the important Imagist periodical *The Egoist*, a best-selling novelist (his *Death of a Hero* recounted his horrifying experiences at the front in France), turned to biography later in his career, producing the first formidable life of D. H. Lawrence, whom he had befriended.

I would call Aldington an anti-establishment biographer— in other words, one akin to myself. Although he was first married to the poet H. D. (Hilda Doolittle) and certainly enjoyed a kind of renown in literary circles, he was practically a recluse by the time he turned to writing biographies. Unlike Boswell and many other biographers, Aldington was no hero-worshiper. The drive to make heroes encourages a mythification of the biographical subject, and Aldington, a demoniac researcher, believed biography should be a bedrock of fact. At one point he wanted to title his biography "Lawrence of Arabia: The Man and the Facts." William Collins, his publisher, disliked the prosaic, rather flat-sounding title and suggested instead the more traditional "Lawrence of Arabia: The Man and the Legend," which Aldington rejected in favor of a more apt one: *Lawrence of Arabia: A Biographical Enquiry*. The subtitle resulted from Aldington's belief that his effort to compose a comprehensive biography had been thwarted at every turn. The best he could do was pose the pertinent questions that someday a biographer would be able to rely on to write a complete life.

Aldington began his work on TEL with no informed point of view. He had not read Lawrence's classic *Seven Pillars of Wisdom*, his account of the Arab revolt, climaxed by his entry into Damascus in 1918 and the defeat of the Turks. Lawrence had long been a celebrated figure in British life when in 1949 a friend of Aldington's first proposed Lawrence of Arabia as a subject likely to interest Aldington and earn him the kind of advance he needed to remain an independent literary man. It is hard to exaggerate the mystique that surrounded Lawrence. He was a Mr. Kurtz who had gone native (dressing in Arab clothing) but who had triumphed as a symbol of enlightened imperialism—making sure the French did not get their filthy hands on the Middle East while liberating a people from Ottoman despotism. Even better, Lawrence seemed to have transcended the Yeatsian dilemma—whether man should opt for perfection of his life or his art. Lawrence, apparently, did not have to choose. He produced a literary masterpiece, and his life itself had the contours of a work of art.

Aldington approached the TEL myth as an agnostic, bemused by the admiring biographies that Robert Graves and Basil Liddell Hart had published and keen to ascertain the basis of their enthusiasm. In less than a year's research (a crack biographer can usually get to the heart of a subject in six months), Aldington began to suspect that Lawrence was a fraud. The biographer scorned Lawrence's self-aggrandizing memoirs and the efforts of his disciples to defend him. Aldington was diffusing the aura of a national hero around whom a literary cult had formed, but whose persona had also been highly burnished by the press and prominent political figures, including Winston Churchill, soon to become prime minister once again.

Aldington understood he was in for trouble. On July 27, 1950, he wrote a friend: "TE is the treasured possession of a clique and much essential information is withheld." Aldington expected TEL's literary executor, his brother, A. W. Lawrence (AWL), to stymie him and the Foreign Office to rebuff his queries. Aldington also expected opposition from the TEL biographers and cheerleaders, who possessed letters and documents that a biographer would obviously wish to examine.

Why didn't Aldington quit right then? Curiously, this is a question that Fred D. Crawford, whose definitive study *Richard Aldington and Lawrence of Arabia: A Cautionary Tale* I rely upon, does not ask. Confronted with such daunting obstacles, most of my fellow biographers would retreat. They would bow out, anticipating attacks on them for proceeding with insufficient sources. Reviewers almost invariably say, "Wait for the authorized biography" as they question the probity of the unauthorized biographer. Most biographers would quit, dreading the moment when the biographical subject's family or friends produce documents contradicting the unauthorized biography. Most biographers would quit because they fear that once bloodied, their subsequent work would not find a publisher or sympathetic reviewers.

Aldington did not because he hated cant and cover-ups. He refused to withdraw because he needed the money, and TEL was a provocative subject likely to attract significant sales. Why critics like Kakutani find this motive unseemly (making money) is beyond me. She does not write for free (I presume) or shy away from controversial subjects or from impugning biographers' motives. She has it easy compared to the biographer, for a controversial biography, unlike a provocative newspaper article, is treated as a kind of ticking bomb that involves the biographer in all kinds of struggles with his own publisher—not to mention all the others who, in Aldington's words, wanted to kill his book.

Quite aside from the temperament of the biographer who forges ahead no matter what is an idea of biography that eludes most critics. Biography is not merely a matter of having access to all the primary sources. Biography is about narrative—presenting a compelling interpretation that even the later discovery of missing facts will not countermand. Biography is about asking the right questions. If the biographer has a compelling vision of the subject, later biographers will confirm and add details, but they will not dislodge an Aldington. This he knew.

The Aldington approach works especially well with subjects who are icons—self-invented figures whose biographies are always more complex and ultimately more interesting than their legend. As Crawford reports, by the end of 1950 Aldington sensed that TEL's admirers were "hiding something, but he had no idea what that might be or even whether it was significant."

Aldington had trouble lining up interviewees: "Now directly I approach somebody they know it is a biographer and are cagey or busy." I can't tell you how many times I've gotten the "busy" line. For some reason, show-business people favor that brush-off. They don't ignore letters; they actually reply (or usually have an assistant call). Thus Mike Nichols was "too busy" to talk about Susan Sontag, and ditto for Richard Attenborough (whose assistant called me to say that Dickie was just too involved with other things to discuss his friend Jill Craigie). This is polite if disingenuous. Dickie is a big talker, so his friends told me, and liked nothing more than to reminisce. His dodging me had other reasons. Biographies are not built in a day, and even the busiest of people set aside a little time when they wish to. Literary figures often do not even acknowledge letters or are quite rude. Biographers, in their view, are at best second rate. Those who do cooperate are usually circumspect because they cannot control the biographer and do not want to suffer the fate of William Styron.

Aldington had to contend with the lot: from artists to politicians to military historians to journalists—most of whom had spent decades lionizing TEL. An especially tough case was Lowell Thomas, the American reporter figure who looms large in David Lean's film *Lawrence of Arabia*. Thomas filmed, photographed, and wrote about Lawrence as if he had been at the great man's side during many of his memorable adventures. Aldington doubted it. He suspected that TEL used Thomas to help project his myth. Crawford reproduces in his book a wonderful photograph of TEL posed as an Arab sheikh. The uncropped image and the draped backdrop make it clear that this shot was taken in Thomas's London flat in

1919, but the cropped image was published to suggest it had been taken in the desert.

Does it matter? Of course, because the picture is posed. It is part of a campaign to position TEL in the same way that Hollywood glamor shots do. It matters because it shows TEL in the process of self-invention. It matters because such photographs are under the control of the subject and his accomplice. It matters because it is not an artifact of history but of fiction.

When my wife and I tried to point out a similar use of photography (especially in jacket photographs) to create the mystique of Susan Sontag, certain reviewers objected. After all, it was her words, not her self-promotion, that really counted. And such would be said about Aldington's exposure of TEL's mythifying. But such objections can be sustained only if they are separated from all the other evidence that a TEL or a Susan Sontag are aiming not simply at achievement but at fame, or at what Leo Braudy calls the "frenzy of renown."

Aldington examined that TEL photograph and began to badger Thomas, attempting to discover whether the reporter had actually witnessed any of TEL's significant triumphs. Aldington understood that Thomas would regard him with great suspicion, and therefore the biographer tried to josh the journalist with opening lines such as "It's me again, damn me," knowing full well that Thomas must already be cursing him. When Thomas did not respond to Aldington's specific questions about his whereabouts during TEL's adventures, the biographer asked him point blank: "Were you with Lawrence on any of the expeditions you describe?" Thomas never answered, and Aldington wrote to a friend, "Of course he wasn't."

Even when a source does not reply, that in itself can be important to the biographer. After all, Thomas had built his early career on describing TEL's exploits. Aldington had what he called an "evil eye," by which he meant a mind that had to be shown proof and would then subject that proof to his merciless gaze.

Biographers build on the silences of the Lowell Thomases of this world. In Aldington's case, his suspicions led him to discovering not only that TEL had been Thomas's main source, but that TEL had written portions of Robert Graves's and Basil Liddell Hart's biographies of him. And what TEL had not written himself, he had vetted. This is what might be called the Thomas Hardy ploy, so eloquently described in Michael Millgate's *Testamentary Acts*. Hardy wrote his autobiography, put his wife's name on it, and called it a biography.

In early 1951, Aldington wrote his publisher to give him fair warning that the biography would be quite contentious, given that Aldington had discovered that TEL had been illegitimate and a homosexual—facts that a few of his intimates suspected but that had not been made public knowledge, especially since TEL's mother was still alive, not to mention two of his brothers. But publishers usually do not quake (in my experience) until they get that first threatening letter, fax, or phone call from the biographical subject's estate or from attorneys representing the subject.

Since the publisher did not withdraw, Aldington persevered. Although he worried and complained about his adversaries, I have no doubt that he also enjoyed the thrill of the hunt and the possession of forbidden knowledge. He had a grasp of TEL that his own brother and literary executor, AWL, did not have, largely because AWL did not consider the kinds of penetrating questions a self-respecting biographer must entertain. "I know things about his brother he doesn't know," Aldington reported. This is no boast. Biographers make a study of their subject; we do not ordinarily do that with friends or family.

Early on, Aldington reached the same conclusion I have always come to while doing unauthorized biographies: don't deal with the subject's estate, which will use the copyright act to censor a manuscript. The estate will demand to see the biographer's book and refuse his request to quote from the subject's work unless the biographer agrees to make certain changes in interpretation that often water down the book; sometimes estates demand that certain passages be cut. Copyright, in other words, intended to protect the theft of an author's words, has been wielded as a weapon against biographers.

Realizing that AWL and other TEL supporters would refuse Aldington permission to quote from TEL's writings, the biographer opted for that apposite subtitle: "A Biographical Enquiry." This is what biographers always do when confronted with a paucity of evidence: write a work that becomes a kind of adventure story relating how the biographer attempted to determine the full story. Thus we have not only the classic *Quest for Corvo* but also *In Search of J. D. Salinger*. This is called making a virtue of necessity. I used a similar tactic in the prologue to *Nothing Ever Happens to the Brave: The Story of Martha Gellhorn*.

Aldington also made a virtue of necessity when he turned to secondary sources, the memoirs and histories written by TEL's contemporaries who served with him in the same theater of war. Aldington found considerable firsthand testimony that disputed TEL's importance in defeating the Turks. Consult Crawford for a stunning summary of how effectively Aldington was able to deflate many of TEL's claims to fame. In a sense, Aldington constructed his own archive, reaching into Arab sources that British biographers had overlooked or discounted.

The unauthorized biographer must work harder than the one who has an estate's blessing. Barred from consulting Lillian Hellman's papers at the University of Texas (they were the exclusive fiefdom of her authorized biographer who never published his book), I reconstructed much of the archive by consulting Ph.D. dissertations produced by scholars working in her archive for almost two decades before Hellman decided to close it down for her handpicked man, the late William Abrahams.

There is, of course, a danger in becoming so zealous against the establishment that the biographer loses perspective, interpreting every bit of evidence to fit his view of his subject's fraudulent behavior. Aldington certainly fell into this trap on occasion, so that a friend would write that after all TEL had some merit: "surely he *was* a remarkable man." Of course Aldington had to shatter the sentimental view of TEL, but his friend cautioned: "Do not hoe into him too hard." The biographer regarded TEL's exploits as a sideshow to the main war in Europe. Thus he wrote about the "national hero of the Great War he never saw." Referring to TEL's writer-friends, Aldington wrote about "people influential in the small but unpleasant literary world." Aldington's publisher edited out his acerbic asides.

The admonition reminded me of Alane Mason, who edited *Susan Sontag: The Making of an Icon*, the biography I wrote with my wife. The first draft disturbed her. It seemed that there were too many instances where we did not consider events from Sontag's point of view, so that it looked as though we were not fair. Alane gave good advice, and we revised accordingly. Aldington's friends kept advising him that he would actually hurt his case if he produced only an indictment. Aldington was on sounder ground when he described TEL as an Irishman who loved telling stories about himself. He loved "mystifying people, and admits that he 'kidded' so perpetually that he didn't himself know where truth ended and fiction began."

Icons often have the Irishman's trouble. Susan Sontag, for example, never stopped telling the fairy tale about how she walked into the offices of Farrar, Straus and Giroux, plopped down the manuscript of her first novel, and walked out only to be thrilled days later when the legendary editor Robert Giroux invited her to lunch and offered her a contract. Nothing like this happened, of course, as Giroux himself specified in a playful letter to her. She had conducted a concerted campaign to get his attention. Again, does it matter? After all, he found the novel publishable. It matters because the biographical subject is presenting an account of a world that does not exist, of events that did not happen as the subject tells them. Writers do not become icons by accident. But Sontag told her fairy tale so often that it seems she believed it. The acting teacher Lee Strasberg once said about his most famous student, "Marilyn Monroe was a dream of Marilyn Monroe."

Aldington confronted another obstacle that biographers in America rarely worry about. As he wrote to Alan Bird, who helped him research TEL's life:

> I have been re-reading the law of libel, and it seems to me that almost any slightly critical statement will be "defamatory" in English law, and as the law presumes that "publication" implies that the writer intended malice and that it has damaged the plaintiff . . . ! I don't think people realize how the law of libel and law of "obscenity" have been carefully warped during the last 150 years to act as a hidden censorship of books.

In English law the onus is on the author and publisher to prove they have *not* committed a libel. In America the onus is on the plaintiff to prove the libel. That is why very few libel cases are brought against biographers in the United States and why controversial biographies are not published in England because publishers do not wish to incur the expense of a trial. Thus my first biography of Martha Gellhorn could not find a British publisher because she threatened to sue. And a threat is enough in most cases. Samuel Johnson would never have been permitted to write so critically about the woman Richard Savage claimed was his mother if the current English libel laws had been in effect then. Aldington dreaded the moment when attorneys would pick apart every phrase that might be construed as libeling a living figure (the dead cannot be libeled).

Lawyers, Aldington knew, would cut a biography to shreds, since it was their job to remove even the remotest possibility of a lawsuit. That is what publishers hire lawyers to do. Aldington called his publisher's lawyers stupid—and so they are from the biographer's point of view. While vetting my Gellhorn manuscript in 1989, an attorney, a Harvard Law graduate, peered at me and asked, "Franklin Roosevelt is dead, isn't he?" She worried that some obscure unnamed person Gellhorn had described during a Caribbean trip in the 1940s might be alive, recognize himself in the text, and sue. My only defense was to rely on my wife, a lawyer with a Ph.D. in English with a special interest in literary properties, libel, and copyright. In two cases (the Hellman and Mailer biographies), her strong arguments dissuaded my publisher from seeking other legal advice. I have no doubt that if these books had been vetted, some of the best passages would have been junked.

That Aldington regarded himself as engaging in a bloodsport is apparent in the phrase he invented for the TEL contingent: "the Lawrence Bureau." They were the equivalent of today's spinmeisters and quick-reaction teams that respond to or even preempt news they deem is derogatory to their candidate. An American biographer might refer instead to the Sontag lobby.

An anti-establishment biographer who understands the forces gunning for him must show that earlier accounts of his subject are suspect because the subject has controlled them. Thus Aldington could be assured of alienating not only earlier biographers but also everyone who had read those books and cherished TEL's heroism. I sympathize with Aldington because of my own discovery that virtually every interview Susan Sontag gave had been vetted and often rewritten by her. The most notorious case is the *Paris Review* interview, which like others in the series is really a disguised autobiography. In the few instances when interviewers somehow eluded her firm hand, Sontag or her publisher protested vehemently.

Those who oppose unauthorized biography view it as a realm of evil retreat, where their cherished icons are maligned. Aldington, on the other hand, wondered what had happened to free speech. One of his opponents, Eric Kennington, wrote to Basil Liddell Hart, Aldington's chief antagonist: "I think you know Aldington has put the Lawrence book in his 'Who's Who' list as 'The book Winston Churchill and others tried to suppress.'" Like today's quick-reaction teams, Liddell Hart had his talking points—a list of criticisms he sent to Aldington's publisher and to prospective reviewers. A military historian, Liddell Hart set up what Crawford calls a "center of intelligence and operations for the anti-Aldington forces." This is no hyperbole. Liddell Hart would hound Aldington to the day of publication and even afterward. After all, Aldington had gone a long way toward exposing Liddell Hart's own bogus TEL biography. Aldington understood that these men would rush to save TEL from the "disgrace of me."

Both Liddell Hart and Robert Graves were in a perilous position, having admitted to each other (as Crawford shows) that TEL had written portions of their books and that they had been disturbed by many discrepancies in their subject's accounts of his heroic behavior. It became imperative to discredit Aldington. Both Liddell Hart and Graves stood to profit monetarily as well (the former having sold the movie rights to his TEL biography, and TEL having provided financial assistance to the latter). Such is the world of mixed motives, for both biographers and subjects. While Lowell Thomas would deplore Aldington's biography in public, here is what he wrote in private to Liddell Hart: "Alas, I guess I was young, rather naïve, and took him [TEL] too literally. At any rate, the yarns that were told were far from true, although I did make several mistakes which have bothered me down through the years."

If Aldington had a harsh penchant for cutting the hero down to size (one reviewer would later say that he hated both TEL and his biographer), his biography, as Crawford amply demonstrates, has stood the test of time, and his adversaries have not. As Adrian Liddell Hart admitted in diplomatic fashion to Crawford, his father "felt strongly about personal friendships and loyalties, transcending other loyalties, and this led him on occasions to disregard interests—and facts." To Graves, Liddell Hart himself confessed that he had perhaps skipped too lightly over TEL's "questionable aspects." Why? As Crawford explains, Liddell Hart believed in TEL's kind of guerilla warfare, his skirmishing that the military historian took as evidence of "indirect war," which often succeeded better than pitched battles. This view had suffered a tremendous loss of prestige after Hitler smashed through the vaunted Maginot Line, which Liddell Hart had touted. By defending TEL, he was also trying to rehabilitate his own reputation.

But Liddell Hart, like so many opponents of unauthorized biographies, went way beyond criticism. As the military historian Jay Luvaas suggested, Liddell Hart was "temperamentally incapable of letting ideas make their own way in the marketplace. . . . He was almost incapable of admitting error." In other words, as Aldington always suspected, Liddell Hart & Co. were out to kill his book—and they almost did, even sending a petition to Elizabeth II asking her to intervene. If the petition failed, all England failed, wrote one demented TEL partisan.

Robert Graves's role in the Stop Aldington movement seems even more despicable than Liddell Hart's. "I think the first action to take against Aldington is to get him on copyright," Graves advised Liddell Hart. Even if publication should not be halted in the United States, Graves was sure, as he wrote to Liddell Hart, they could "lay on" reviews. But Aldington foiled such a strategy by minimizing quotations and using what the British call "fair dealing," or "fair use" in American terminology, which allows a writer to paraphrase and summarize his subject's words for purposes of critical comment.

As part of the campaign against Aldington, AWL reissued in truncated form *T. E. Lawrence by His Friends*. As Aldington observed to a friend, "they have cut out the parts I proved are lies!" Nevertheless the shorter edition was "an effective Lawrence bureau riposte," Crawford concludes.

Aldington found his publisher no use at all. Collins had been attracted by the sales he thought a controversial book would generate, but like most publishers he blanched at the threat of legal action and even turned over the manuscript to Liddell Hart for his comments! One editor at Collins wrote Liddell Hart that they had gone to "very great trouble to make the book as inoffensive as we can." In the end, Collins did not back down from publishing the book, but in the meantime he gave Aldington's enemies more than two years to concert their forces. I felt much the same way when W. W. Norton gave Sontag's attorney Martin Garbus a copy of the Sontag biography. When I asked why, I was told it was because Norton felt it had "nothing to hide." As if that were the point! Garbus had already tried to intimidate my agent into handing over the manuscript. When that did not work, he tried Norton—already softened up by the belligerent Roger Straus, who claimed that Norton, because it was Farrar, Straus's competitor, was merely trying to annoy him by publishing a biography of one of his star writers. Like Collins, Norton ultimately stood by the biography, but it certainly allowed Sontag & Co. the time to line up interviews and articles that heaped scorn on the biography my wife and I had written.

Aldington was able to anticipate the list of reviewers who would try to annihilate his book. He knew the biography book-reviewing business well, and, as Crawford comments, the biographer was prophetic: "almost everyone on the list either appeared in print to oppose the book before publication or defended TEL against Aldington" in the storm of controversial reviews that broke even before the book officially appeared on January 31, 1955.

Paul Johnson was the rare reviewer who saw what was at stake:

> It now looks as though Mr. Aldington's biography of Lawrence of Arabia will not survive the malevolent and well-directed barrage of criticism which it provoked. The English literary establishment, having failed to kill the book before birth, has slaughtered it in early infancy. Nevertheless, it has largely

achieved its purpose. Those of us who read it and were not already prejudiced in Lawrence's favour, now find it impossible to regard him with anything except contemptuous tolerance.

Johnson well understood the dynamic of book reviewing and the fate of unauthorized biographies. Crawford points out that three-quarters of the reviews were negative. Aldington attributed much of this reaction to *him*. I wish he were alive so that I could say to him, "You should not have taken it so personally. If you review the reception of similar unauthorized works, you will find that three-quarters negative is the customary proportion." In other words, any biographer who attempts to do an Aldington is likely to meet the same fate. The three-quarters proportion is archetypal; it is in the nature of what happens to unauthorized biographers of the Aldington stripe.

I have tried to explain this fact to friends and colleagues who are also writing unauthorized biographies. Eudora Welty's biographer, Ann Waldron, had received almost nothing but accolades for her earlier biographies of Caroline Gordon and Hodding Carter. She was stunned at the vitriol heaped on her Welty work. My dear friend the late Carole Klein never got over the hostility that greeted her biography of Doris Lessing. Only Marion Meade, I believe, had hardened herself to put up with the acrimony caused by her Woody Allen biography. None of these biographers had earlier received such a drubbing, and even though they had seen me bloodied by reviews, I could tell from a remark Ann made that she thought (but was too polite to say so) that the negative reviews had something to do with *me*. In *Telling Women's Lives: The New Biography*, Linda Wagner-Martin, an esteemed literary critic, explains that she was astounded to discover her integrity impugned when she published a biography of Sylvia Plath. Was she really the awful person described in her reviews? she asked family and friends.

Conversely, my life of Rebecca West, which began as an unauthorized work but evolved into one that my subject's family endorsed, received the best reviews (and also enjoyed the poorest sales) of all my seven biographies. Had I suddenly gotten religion? Become a better biographer? I don't believe so. I had simply written a book that suited the mind-set of reviewers.

Although Paul Johnson spoke of Aldington's slaughter, in a way he also acknowledged that the biographer had triumphed. Although Aldington would get precious little credit for doing so (except from the Fred Crawfords of the world), he had shifted the terms of the discussion. He had made way for later biographies that would portray TEL in a more accurate and perceptive light.

The argument that biographies such as Aldington's can harm a subject in any significant way—call it the Graves-digging school of anti-biography—is fallacious. Since Aldington, admiring biographies of TEL continue to be published, though now they have to take into account a much more complex set of factors, thanks again to Aldington.

Aldington found the wording in the negative reviews so uniform that he became suspicious. Rightly so. Liddell Hart had a distribution list that went out to reviewers. Crawford shows that in two cases the reviews—by Graves and David Garnett—were based not on a reading of Aldington's biography but on Liddell Hart's talking points. How can Crawford be so sure? Because the passages Graves and Garnett attack are not in Aldington's published book; rather, they belong to an earlier draft that Aldington's publisher had shown Liddell Hart.

The Graves and Garnett duo reminded me of Christopher Hitchens, a Sontag confidant, who attacked our Sontag biography in *Vanity Fair* before the book was published. He latched on to not a draft of the book but merely a draft of the publisher's hyperbolic description of the biography. That magazine had considered publishing an excerpt from the Sontag biography but backed off not because of Sontag's antagonism but because her significant other, the photographer Annie Leibovitz, was one of their star contributors whom they did not wish to alienate. Another magazine also dropped its interest in publishing an excerpt and instead wrote about Sontag and her new novel, *In America*.

First-serial sales (excerpts that appear before book publication) help unauthorized biographers get to readers before the critics begin their demolition campaigns. Aldington had hoped to have leverage with his book publisher by setting up a newspaper serialization, but not even the tabloids would publish, given the legal rumblings of the Lawrence bureau.

Reviewers dismissed Aldington as a "professional denigrator"—an extraordinary way to treat an important literary figure. Even the one-quarter of reviewers who tried to give Aldington a fair hearing came out sounding regretful that the biographer had made the effort: "Lawrence was a splendid and gallant adventurer who brought colour and inspiration into our lives at a time when we sadly needed both, and it is tragic that the adulation of his friends should have driven a costive penman into a paroxysm of debunking a rather vulnerable hero." The revealing sense of regret helps to explain why Aldington was treated as a spoilsport. "Susan Sontag is a lesbian!" said my wife's friend's husband. He expressed the shock that anyone feels who has been misled and formed all sorts of assumptions that are incorrect. But Sontag became a more interesting figure, not less, because of the revelation—which was certainly no revelation at all to the literary establishment. Yet everyone thought a biography publishing the facts would be daring and perhaps even marked for a lawsuit. As soon as the biography appeared, however, Sontag quickly adapted to the new set of facts and artfully and even casually dealt with a subject that heretofore dared not speak its name.

My unauthorized biographies have not resulted in difficulties obtaining work, but there are repercussions. Thus in *Sontag and Kael*, Craig Seligman refers to a "hostile, inept biography" which offered only gossip about her sex life. The critic does not give the biography's title, because to do so would be to negate his point. The book contained virtually no gossip and was about—as the subtitle made clear—the "making of an icon." In a sense the Sontag biography was a "biographical enquiry" much like Aldington's, since my wife and I made no pretense of writing anything like a complete life. Reviewers, however, angry about the very idea of such a biography, failed to make distinctions.

That reviewers did not wish to take seriously the idea of an icon suggests to me how much of an icon Sontag is. Norman Podhoretz once called her the "dark lady of American letters," suggesting that only one woman per generation could earn such a title, that the culture had room for only one. Before Sontag it was Mary McCarthy. This is what Aldington's reviewer meant by calling TEL a figure who supplied color and inspiration to a society that sorely needed both. Sontag's fairy tales have projected her as a similar inspirational and formidable figure. Her hijinks remind me of Lord Vansittart's dismissal of TEL's aggrandizing: "Everyone was indeed potty about this flood-lit man, who deserved his Bath and Distinguished Service Order but nothing like apotheosis."

Even after an Aldington, the myth lives on. TEL's older brother, M. R. Lawrence, refused to believe that he and his brothers were illegitimate. Not even documents, sometimes, can budge true believers. When I discovered that Jill Craigie was born in 1911, not 1914 as she maintained, Michael Foot refused to believe me. "But the correct date is on two passports," I showed him. "Mistakes," was his terse reply. "But the 1911 date is on her death and birth certificates," I continued. He shook his head. For more than forty-five years he had believed he was two years older than she. Who was I, a mere biographer, to correct the record? Even Liddell Hart had to believe Aldington about TEL's illegitimacy, yet he spent a futile four hours trying to convince M. R. Lawrence that it was so.

It was small consolation to Aldington that C. P. Snow wrote in *The Nation* that while the establishment rallied against the biographer in public, in private they were now suggesting that Aldington had it about 85 percent right. One of Jill's friends told me, "I knew about the correct date, but I thought you should find it out for yourself." Like TEL, Jill concealed much about her early years. When a friend of hers read a draft of my biography, she remarked: "Now I understand why Jill always changed the subject when I asked about herself."

The greatest irony is that those who build on the unauthorized biographer's work continue to discredit him. Thus Terence Rattigan's play about TEL, *Ross*, borrowed a good bit from Aldington even as the playwright wrote to AWL dissociating himself from the unauthorized rogue: "God, I hate him,"

Rattigan claimed. This repudiation of Aldington did not deter AWL from finding the play, too, hostile to his brother.

The villainous Robert Graves tried to sue Rattigan for copyright infringement of Graves's biography. But the flimsy case went nowhere even as AWL tried to control the portrayal of his brother in David Lean's film and in other projects—showing again that it was not Aldington per se but anyone's effort to be independent that proved a problem to the Lawrence bureau.

In biography as a bloodsport it is only the unauthorized biographer's motivations that are subjected to merciless scrutiny. The exceptions to that generalization are very few. Indeed, they practically begin and end with *Keepers of the Flame*, *Testamentary Acts*, and Crawford's invaluable book, which, as he states in the preface, is a

> "cautionary tale" about the precarious position of an author who presumes to challenge the established view of a national hero, the extensive legal means available to those who can afford to force a publisher to alter or suppress a manuscript, and the ability of an influential coterie to damage the reputation of a book even before people have had a chance to read it. The nearly successful attempts to suppress Aldington's book reveal how little freedom of the press can mean when a book displeases or discomfits influential people with positions—or myths—to maintain.

After the relentless attacks on Aldington, it is startling to read Crawford's assessment of the authorized biography, which appeared in 1989: "It left Aldington comparatively unscathed." This was exactly my conclusion when Caroline Moorehead's authorized biography of Martha Gellhorn appeared: more detail, to be sure, but no essential alteration in the picture.

Biography is often accused of confusing literature and life. Yet Aldington shows that figures like TEL are literary creations, personas; it is the literary idolaters who confuse the image for the real thing. Or as the biographer Michael Holroyd said, biography prevents us from becoming too bookish.

If TEL deserved his "Bath," as Lord Vansittart acknowledged, then I propose Richard Aldington for the Order of the Bloodbath.

SINCE MODERNISM has elevated the literary work as a religious text, it is no wonder that the biographer as Judas becomes such a compelling metaphor. Biography has come to be regarded as an attack on literature itself. Consequently biographers like Ellmann have had to overcome the kind of initial resistance Harriet Shaw Weaver put up. I'll never forget the late Frederick Karl's advice: Write several works of literary criticism first. That is the way to establish your reputation in the academy, the way to show critics you are serious about literature. Then write biographies if you must.

Ian Hamilton thought that after his more or less authorized biography of Robert Lowell, he could finesse an unauthorized biography of J. D. Salinger. The reclusive author, enveloped in mystique since he secluded himself in Cornish, New Hampshire, in the early 1950s and then withdrew into himself even further by the mid-1960s, refusing all interviews and declining to cooperate with articles about him, was the kind of subject publishers salivate over. Salinger himself, who hated publishers as much as biographers, knew this as well. In retrospect it is apparent that Hamilton was taking on not merely a writer who objected to a biography of him but who objected to biography, period. I have a special sympathy for Hamilton, because Martha Gellhorn adopted much the same position, forcing me, like Hamilton, to question the very nature of the genre.

Hamilton, a poet and editor well versed in the ways of the literary world, gun-shy from the wounds suffered during his bout with Lowell's circle, thought the Salinger project "might at moments seem bracingly unmessy"—as he remarks in *In Search of J. D. Salinger*. In the end, however, it was all mess, resulting in court battles, the constant rewriting of his book, and a legal judgment that radically changed the kind of biography he published. His title says it all. Like Aldington's "biographical enquiry," Hamilton's "in search of" is the biographer's attempt to make do with limited access, not merely to sources but to the very words he would have liked to reproduce in order to render the flavor of his subject's life.

Hamilton turned to Salinger, he explains, because even the authorized biographer has to deal with the "unpleasant aspects" of his role:

> For all that you enjoyed this magic-sounding right of access, you still had to be endlessly judging and rejudging limits of propriety. And to some extent you were always having to play one witness off against another. There were too many tightropes, too many injurable sensitivities, and later, when the book was done, too many denials and recriminations. Lowell had been loved by several people, but few of these people loved or even liked each other. And yet all of them believed that their version of the man was the authentic one—it had to be because their love, which they knew to be authentic, made it so.

This splendid passage puts you smack into the biographer's place, showing why the biographer—even when he is not blocked by sources—is likely to take some body blows.

I have done two more or less authorized biographies, of Rebecca West and Jill Craigie, but I have always returned to unauthorized biography because it is the only way to be your own man. Even if the authorized biographer is not bludgeoned by those who believe their version of the subject is the authentic one, he or she must remain on guard, engaging in the delicate diplomacy of staying "in the family," so to speak—that is, convincing your sources that you share their sentiments even as you oh so carefully hint that the biographer has other considerations (interpretations). "What if you and Michael [Foot] disagree on a point?" one of his relatives asked me. "Then it's my call, and he kicks me out of the house," I joked. I tried to josh my way through this sticky path, but in the end it was no laughing matter, because my Jill was not precisely the Jill he knew.

Salinger would be less messy because Hamilton would be beholden to no one. He could write a crisp, uncluttered narrative because he would not have access to everything. This is a virtue that almost no critic of biography appreciates—indeed, most biographers do not understand the principle. Hamilton is one of the few who seems to understand an aspect of biography that I have been mining for much of my career.

Leon Edel complained that modern biographers are prisoners of the archive; they must learn to be more selective. In a sense, the unauthorized biography imposes limits—a certain discipline on the biographer. He cannot take refuge in detail; he cannot be misguided by it. Or as Hamilton puts it, "there was little chance that I would become bewildered by a surfeit of material."

Although critics complain about doorstop biographies (the very phrase my London editor employed when he received the first draft of my Rebecca West manuscript), they attack the unauthorized biographer because he has not had "access" to enough details. The critics' celebration of access is fallacious in two respects. First, access does not equal complete control over the material or even comprehensiveness. The industrious unauthorized biographer will discover treasures because he has to. Hamilton turned up several hundred Salinger letters in the course of his research—as I did, for example, in working on my Hellman biography, which also resulted in discovering a screenplay she never mentioned and that no other researcher had located.

Second, and more important, the unauthorized biographer can often see the subject whole because he works inductively, finding choice examples of his subject's character that are more evocative than the minutely documented deductive life.

Judging by *In Search of J. D. Salinger*, however, I do not believe that Hamilton saw his advantages clearly enough. The subliminal message I detect in his rueful and often comic narrative is that deep down he hoped—perhaps even expected—eventually to secure Salinger's cooperation, if not authorization. Without the crutch of authorization, Hamilton floundered in spite of the brave face he put on his undertaking.

The question is why? Why did Hamilton delude himself? Why did Salinger turn out to be the bloodiest opponent a biographer can imagine? The biographer proposed his biography without a definite idea of what he could accomplish. Do I have now, right now, enough material to write a biography of the subject? Is there a bedrock of fact? Of course I hope for some lucky breaks and discoveries, but what is my base? In Hellman's case it was those Ph.D. dissertations and several archives that would be open to me even though her Texas repository had shut its doors. The same was true for Gellhorn. And for Sontag, it was my awareness that her publisher's archive at the New York Public Library would not only be open to me but that my wife and I would be the first biographers to read her correspondence.

Hamilton began his biography as an act of homage. In his youth he had been entranced by *Catcher in the Rye*. He loved that book and held a reverence for it that a whole generation of readers shared—including my first wife, who had read the novel thirteen times by the age of eighteen. As Hamilton puts it, "For many months . . . I went around being Holden Caulfield. I carried his book everywhere with me as a kind of talisman." Notice the pronoun suggests that Caulfield, not Salinger, wrote the book. In other words, Holden Caulfield was not merely a character but a real person. The irony is that Hamilton would learn that Salinger thought of Caulfield in the same way, as if the character had written the book. This turns the novel—turns literature itself—into a living entity over which the biographer and his subject are prone to conflict.

To me, Hamilton was not sufficiently cold-blooded. He never saw Salinger clearly as a subject, the product of a book. Biography as book is not biography as life—an obvious distinction—yet both biographers and critics seem bemused that book biographies have limitations. But these limitations are what allow biography as a genre to grow, with biographies of the same subject building on one another.

Hamilton was canny enough not to promise too much in his book proposal. He suggested he would write a book like the *Quest for Corvo*, presenting the biographer as an adventurer attempting to penetrate the mystique of his subject. In the end he did write such a book, but only after legal action forced him to do so. But that is to anticipate. What I wish to point out here is that from the very moment the biographer wrote to the subject, he was already recasting his ambition, dreaming that Salinger would come round to his pitch.

In his letter to Salinger, Hamilton presented himself as a critical biographer, that is, one who was serious about the life and the work. With so little reliable information about Salinger, it was time to set the record straight. Hamilton knew, of course, that Salinger had been approached this way many times, and that Hamilton's own letter was "entirely disingenuous." Salinger wanted no record; he despised the very notion of literary biography.

Hamilton says he never expected Salinger to answer the letter. Indeed, the biographer wanted to be free of his subject's control in order to write a "semispoof in which the biographer would play a leading, sometimes comic, role." This is what Hamilton eventually wrote, but I have trouble believing that he did not yearn for Salinger's acknowledgment, as readers do when they write to their beloved authors.

It seems to me that as soon as Salinger did reply, Hamilton went off the rails. Even though the subject rejected the idea of biography and felt it was just a form of harassment, he also said he supposed he could not prevent Hamilton from writing a book about him. This kind of reply is, to the biographer, a form of encouragement. At least a dialogue has begun—or so the biographer thinks, as my wife and I did when we received a cheery letter from Sontag's agent, Andrew Wylie, wanting to know what kind of book we were writing and what sources we planned to consult. That depended, we replied, on whether or not Sontag wished to cooperate. No more was heard from that quarter, but it was some time before we disabused ourselves of the idea that she just might be sporting enough to engage us.

Ditto for Hamilton, who was amazed not only to receive a reply from Salinger's agent but an invitation to meet. Hamilton showed Salinger's letter to friends. One interpreted his "I can't stop you" as "Please go ahead." There were other, less encouraging interpretations, but, as Hamilton confesses, he had accepted an advance and had already spent a good portion of it, and the response from Salinger now made him real to the biographer in a new way. The subject was now a presence, not just an idea, in the biographer's life.

The avid biographer paused briefly to mull over Salinger's right to privacy. Was it the same as anyone else's? Yes, the biographer answered, "but then again, not quite." Was Salinger different from other world-famous authors whose lives intrigued their readers? "Who does he think he is?" one of Hamilton's friends asked. Why had Salinger made such a fetish of his privacy? "What's *your* game?" Hamilton the biographer asked.

If Hamilton had stuck to that question—that is, shaped a biography around it—he would have saved himself a lot of grief and considerable soul-searching. He could organize details from interviews and archives that showed why Salinger had always been, to one degree or another, a highly creative but anti-social figure, whose view of art ultimately led him to his Cornish redoubt. *In Search of J. D. Salinger* explores that core question inside of an account that reveals Hamilton's failed effort to write a more traditional work.

At the beginning of his research, Hamilton took a wrong turn. He decided to "observe some ground rules. Since up to 1965, he had been in the public domain, but thereafter had elected not to be, I would not pursue my researches beyond that date." Hamilton also decided not to "bother" Salinger's family and friends.

But what is biography but a bother? I can understand why for strategic reasons a biographer would make Hamilton's choices. For example, I decided not to contact Gellhorn's adopted son. He had had a hard time with his mother—as I was able to glean from her own letters—and I knew it would only irritate her further to call on him. But I never dreamed that my restraint would convince her of "what was possible, decently possible, in a genre such as this," to quote Hamilton's hopes regarding Salinger.

When I say Hamilton was not cold-blooded enough, I mean to say he still yearned for his subject's approval and for his own. He says as much in his book, but I'm not sure he entirely understood what damage he did to himself by attempting to placate his subject. The point is that Hamilton was writing *his* book and thus by definition it could never win Salinger's tolerance, let alone support. There would be a book only because Hamilton wanted one, and that fact was mortally offensive to his subject.

Hamilton had more to worry about than Salinger: "People in New York wanted to know all that could be known about Salinger, this mysterious 'celebrity,' and yet at the same time they evinced a protectiveness toward him, as if his inaccessibility was a national treasure that I, the invader, somehow threatened to despoil." Sometimes the same person would deplore delving into Salinger's life and then give Hamilton a tip about someone who might be willing to talk about the sacred subject.

Hamilton admits to more than a little confusion himself. He wanted to draw a line, a border around the subject, one that would define the extent to which the biographer could trespass on privacy. Writers themselves gave indications of how much of their privacy they wished to preserve, Hamilton argued with friends. In other words, it was a case-by-case problem. This may be so for the subjects of biography, but for biographers? Hamilton fell back on the lame excuse that Salinger's work was "more than usually powered by autobiography." Salinger himself had implied as much in his own fiction. But as Salinger would respond, that is for him to say. Hamilton would be on better ground simply to reiterate the difference between autobiography and biography. If there is to be one, there has to be the other—yin and yang.

The biographer's invasiveness is so troublesome to Hamilton that he splits himself in two, carrying on a dialogue in *In Search of J. D. Salinger* between the part of himself that is the gumshoe seeking every fact and clue without scruple and the literary man still trying to make fine distinctions about what is and what is not fair game. These dialogues are fun and reveal much about the qualms biographers entertain and are rarely honest about. But this splitting in two is a fiction. There was one Ian Hamilton, and once he got onto Salinger's trail he wanted to know everything, not just enough to do his *Quest for Corvo*. How could the biographer not be regarded as a kind of monster?

To continue with a Salinger-like project, the biographer has to harden himself. One way to do that is to become suspicious. The subject is hiding something—this is the line that many of Hamilton's friends took, the one I have heard countless times when I explain to friends that my subject is uncooperative. We all have something to hide, I suppose, but the response is just too facile. Most people believe they own their own lives, and many of them would be aghast at the idea of someone else writing them up. If people are surprised at how their recorded voices sound, or they say a photograph does not really look like them, what would they make of a biography of themselves? My friends—even my agent—have said the subject ought to be flattered. Spend a few weeks researching a biography, prying into lives, and the idea of biography as flattery vanishes. The novelist Samuel Delany reminded me in a letter that the subject's desire to defend himself is easily misconstrued: "The gesture that protects is also and always equally a gesture than can be construed as hiding something."

Hamilton himself provides a better hardening technique with the question he never had a chance to put to Salinger in person: "What is *your* game?" People in New York told Hamilton, "No one will talk," as if his subject were a "high-placed mobster who had ways of guaranteeing the loyalty of his lieutenants." This is exactly what we went around saying about Sontag: it was like working on a mafia biography.

Hamilton asked himself what he would do if he actually encountered someone close enough to Salinger to "spill the beans." Of course he would listen, the biographer admits. But my jaw drops when Hamilton adds, "But perhaps the first question I would want to put to them would be: Why are you saying this? And what makes you different from the others?" Those would be the last questions I would ask, and only after I was fairly certain all the beans had been spilled.

It is hard for me to see why Hamilton was on safer moral ground when he went about asking questions about Salinger's father, whose business associates kept asking the biographer, "Why don't you ask the boy?" A good question. Did Hamilton duck it? He didn't say. Confronted with similar questions in St. Louis, where I interviewed Gellhorn's schoolmates and childhood friends, I replied that I had written to her and was hoping she would cooperate. I did not say that she had already rebuffed me once, or that I doubted she would come round. There have been occasions (though not in my experience) when reluctant subjects have decided to help biographers. I did not kid myself—not much anyway. I did not believe I was lying but rather was just economical with the truth and reluctant to add to my burdens by providing fuller explanations. No one pressed me. Without knowing more about the nuts and bolts of Hamilton's approach to interviewees, I can only wonder at how he extracted his nuggets.

Rather than focusing on what he can know and how his available material bears on his core theme—why Salinger became so reclusive and how his concept of art actually reinforced his retirement from public life—Hamilton strained to write a conventional biography, trying to fill in gaps with locutions: "no great impertinence to suppose," "it's possible," and "it could have been." All this sort of wishful thinking gives biography a bad name—makes it look, indeed, like an idle sport.

Hamilton longed for the "off-the-record voice of Salinger" and rejoiced when he found a cache of letters at the University of Texas that reveal the callow young writer. Hamilton's quotations from these letters, in particular, is what got the biographer in trouble. He quoted under the "fair use" doctrine, the vague concept that permits brief quotations from published and unpublished work as well as paraphrases without seeking permission from the author or the author's estate. I can see why he clung to them, believing his readers would want to hear Salinger's own voice. And Hamilton had reason to suppose he was on sound legal ground.

Texas permitted Hamilton to take notes but would not photocopy the letters. He had to sign an agreement that stipulated he could not reproduce the material without the library's permission. He was right to be skeptical about the agreement he signed. I have signed dozens of such documents that have no legal standing whatsoever because the library is almost always not the copyright holder. There is no way for a library to bar fair use. As one archivist told me, her library required such signed agreements as a way of placating the donors of the papers. In effect such libraries act as enforcement agencies—in my view a reprehensible role for a library to play. But they depend on donors who can get quite angry when they learn about the uses to which the papers can be put. The library, in effect, puts the biographer on notice while assuring its patrons that everything possible is being done to police the riffraff. There is a funny moment in *In Search of J. D. Salinger* when a horrified Hamilton finds a dozen of his own letters in the Texas collection and exclaims, "Why, anyone could just walk in and . . ."

Hamilton gets to the heart of biography and (for me) the heart of biography as bloodsport when he discovers that early on Salinger could not bear to read what others said about his characters anymore than he liked being asked personal questions. He treated his characters like real people whose privacy and integrity had been violated by literary critics, let alone would-be biographers. Salinger felt a special responsibility to protect his characters, as though they were actually his children. He would take this parental attitude to such an extreme that he would eventually cease publishing altogether. It seems never to have occurred to him that biography and literary criticism are justified precisely because both fictional characters and their creator have to make their way in the world, which inevitably entails the perceptions of others.

Salinger disliked jacket photographs of the author, advance proofs of books, indeed any kind of publicity long before he actually severed his connections with publishers. He lived like an ascetic and adopted a view of literature as a series of sacred texts. He preserved his integrity by remaining aloof from phonies—publishers and biographers especially included. To be alone, in other words, was the only way to remain faithful to his work, to which he devoted himself with a religious fervor.

Hamilton makes the shrewd point that Salinger had to confront what Randall Jarrell called "The Age of Criticism." Writers were now ensconced in colleges, and professors were making an industry out of teaching and writing about modern and contemporary literature. It is revealing that almost all of Salinger's favorite writers had been dead for at least a hundred years. And it was shocking to him when his contemporaries—Norman Mailer, John Updike, Leslie Fiedler, Joan Didion, Alfred Kazin, and Mary McCarthy—all seemed to team up to trash (however politely in some cases) *Franny and Zooey*. This eagerness to make a meal of a contemporary writer revolted him.

Hamilton should have known he was in very deep trouble when he came across the passage in *Seymour: An Introduction* in which Seymour's widow polices the criticism of his work by being very strict about granting permission to quote from it. Like other literary widows and estates, this fictional writer's spouse uses the copyright act as though it were part of the penal code. When I read Hamilton's discussion of *Seymour: An Introduction*, I was amazed that he did not comment on this prophetic passage. John Updike was equally prophetic in his review of *Franny and Zooey* when he remarked that Salinger's characters had become "a hermitage for him."

Salinger had turned his back on the whole literary enterprise, except for the writing of literature itself, which would be done not only privately but would not be published. In *Seymour: An Introduction* he rejected the professionals and sought the "amateur reader," if there were still some "left in the world—or anybody who just reads and runs—I ask him or her, with untellable affection and gratitude, to split the dedication of this book four ways with my wife and children."

That really says it all. The only recourse for the biographer at this point is to inquire again about Salinger's game: How had he come to such a narrow view of the literary life? The irony is that when Salinger took Hamilton to court, alleging copyright infringement in the quotations from his letters, the courts ultimately sided with him—treating his unpublished words as only *his* property. Hamilton was surely right in thinking that quoting two hundred words out of thirty thousand was fair use—a very small borrowing of Salinger's words that would not destroy their commercial value (should Salinger wish to publish his letters), and not a theft that deprived the original author of his distinctive expressiveness.

Hamilton kept revising his book to please Salinger and his lawyers, "still believing that he might rather like my book. He more than anyone would know what I'd left out. He would know which leads I'd elected not to chase after. He would un-destand the book's essential sympathies and warm to them." Even after all his research, Hamilton continued to delude himself. Eventually he understood that it was not this word or that passage, one letter or another, but the "*whole thing*" Salinger objected to.

The Salinger case effectively wiped out fair use in the quotation from unpublished writings. It took a change in the copyright act in 1992 for Congress to restore the notion of fair use that biographers had heretofore thought was theirs to employ—as the Association of American Publishers and the Organization of American Historians made clear when lobbying the national legislature for relief from the courts' restrictive interpretations of fair use.

As Hamilton confesses at the end of *In Search of J. D. Salinger*, he never "properly outgrew" his seventeen-year-old self's infatuation with the subject. The biography Hamilton finally wrote, the "legal version," as he calls it, is as good a fable about the perils of bloodsport biography as we are likely to encounter.

THE SALINGER CASE created a widespread chilling effect in the publishing world. Beacon Press told Louise DiSalvo that she could quote only one hundred words from Virginia Woolf's papers and publications for her *Virginia Woolf: The Impact of Childhood Abuse on Her Life and Work*. My publisher limited me to three of Gellhorn's unpublished words ("hot jungle breath") used to describe Hemingway's malevolent presence in her life—and I had to fight to get that phrase into my biography of her.

Biographical subjects and their estates, with the law now on their side more than ever, were emboldened to feel even more aggrieved against biographers. Their outrage crested with Natasha Spender's "Private and Public Lives," a commentary published in 1992 in the *Times Literary Supplement* (*TLS*). She began by reporting that four of her friends—"all decent, generous, reasonable and truthful people" were sick (one seriously so) because they were about to appear in biographies. Like blackmail targets, these friends had been dreading for years the day when publication would lay them low.

Spender (wife of the poet Stephen Spender) likened the biographers to a "self-appointed judge and jury" who were not bound by rules of evidence. Their subjects merely represented "jackpots" of material. Biographers had refused the subjects' requests to review material before publication. She scorned the biographer's view that such requests only constituted attempts to thwart publication.

In the last decade biographers had drastically overturned "formerly accepted principles," Spender announced. It was now time to revise their code of practice. She had in mind efforts to restrain the ruthless idea that any person of achievement was "fair game" for the biographer. What had happened to the scholar's "intelligent sympathy" for his subject? She named Richard Ellmann as her shining ideal.

An article on biography by John Lahr in the *Evening Standard* had provoked Spender's outcry, for he had called the biographer "ruthlessly disinterested" and equipped to penetrate the myth the subject had made of his life. Spender found this assumption arrogant. Why should the biographer's word be accepted rather than the testimony of those who had known the subject for years?

In Spender's view, the biographer's knowledge is "superficial," just the sum of a few years of delving into the subject's life. Such biographers have no personal or intimate images to conjure up. In short, the biographer's knowledge is secondhand at best. She cites, as an example, Michael Shelden's biography of George Orwell, to which many Orwell friends have objected.

It would be too much to expect Spender to see it from the biographer's perspective, but here is an excerpt from Ann Thwaite's preface to *A. A. Milne: His Life* that helps put Spender's complaint into perspective:

> Clive Bell, Virginia Woolf's brother-in-law, a contemporary of Milne's at Trinity College, Cambridge, wrote in his book *Old Friends* that old friends and relations will always dispute the conclusions of biographers. "Mrs Thrale, who knew Johnson far longer and far more intimately than Boswell knew him, doubtless said as much. And of course Mrs Thrale was right. Only she forgot that it was Boswell's business to write a biography, to depict a man in all his activities and in his relations to all sorts of people, while it was her privilege to record a personal impression." Milne was no Dr Johnson and I am no Boswell, but the principle holds. Those readers who knew a different A. A. Milne from the one they find in this book must bear that in mind.

Biography is a book and a form of knowledge quite different from knowing the biographical subject in the flesh. After reading Richard Holmes's biography of Coleridge, the critic Britte Fraser concluded: "I feel I know him more deeply than I know my friends or even my husband. It is ironic that a rich, detailed biography brings me closer to a person's inwardness than I can hope to achieve in living relationships."

Spender, on the other hand, has experienced biographers only as a criminal class. She describes how they insinuate themselves into their subjects' lives—outlining a letter-writing and interview campaign that jibes at many points with Ian Hamilton's account in *In Search of J. D. Salinger*. Often the biographer has merely made a phone call and obtained little information, but the interviewee's or correspondent's name is added to the burgeoning list in the Acknowledgments section, as if to prove the biographer has been diligent and authoritative. Often the information given is distorted, and despite promises, the biographer does not allow his sources to check their contributions.

Such is the "objective" biography that John Lahr touts, Spender argues. It is a sham that reviewers are in no position to verify or dispute. How are they to know that even the biographer's longer interviews are squeezed into a sentence or two that warps what the witness had to say?

The code of fair dealing that Spender proposes includes showing a list of those who approved of the biographer's use of their contributions, and a list of those who did not. This implies, of course, that every contributor to the book would see it before publication. Spender even goes so far as to say that the contributor's testimony should be copyrighted to guard against its misuse.

But believing that biographical subjects are not yet protected enough, Spender advocates their legal right to grant or deny permission to publish a biography in their lifetimes. To Spender, other concerns about national or public interest could be resolved (no doubt in favor of the subject). In the absence of such a law, however, she stipulates that the biographer and publisher have a moral obligation to consult the subject and to abide by the subject's wishes. Even after the subject's death, a biographer could go ahead only if the literary executors agreed, Spender adds. Only toward the end of her commentary does Spender acknowledge her anger over Hugh David's proposed biography of her husband, which Mrs. Spender had found grossly inaccurate.

Although unauthorized biography appears to be Spender's target, in fact the idea of biography itself, I would argue, is really what upsets her. Even the sainted Ellmann, she reports, had regrets about publishing "very private letters of James Joyce." I do not know the source of Spender's comment, but it does not agree with my reading of Ellmann's archive or of his practice as a biographer. Just the contrary, I would say, is true. And though Spender chides biographers about not revealing all their sources, she gives no indication of where or when Ellmann expressed his regret. Everything I know about Ellmann suggests that he would have been appalled by Spender's efforts to regulate biographers.

At the very bottom of this *TLS* commentary came the announcement: "Peter Parker will review *Stephen Spender: A Portrait with Background* in next week's *TLS*." This statement gives the lie to Spender's suggestion that she and her friends are helpless victims. The *TLS* not only provided her with a forum, it had made sure to publish her piece before Hugh David's book appeared. Reviewers savaged David's book throughout the British press. So much for Spender's view that biographical subjects are helpless.

In the literary world, in particular, subjects and their estates control the flow of information, so that Spender's portrayal of the reckless biographer riding shotgun is ludicrous. If biographers had been as irresponsible as she supposes, there would have been lawsuits galore, especially in England where the law favors subjects and their estates. The idea that the 1980s were somehow an especially free-riding reign for biographers who willy-nilly invaded their subjects' privacy is a fantasy.

I have before me the PEN Newsletter of October 1963, which recounts a panel discussion entitled "Is Biography an Invasion of Privacy?" Leon Edel seemed to take umbrage at the very question and blustered that he was tired of being asked about how Henry James "felt about men and women . . . about love. What James's physical amatory activities were is certainly not my business . . . nor anyone else's!" When asked if James had a sex life, Edel replied, "I don't know nor do I care!"

Kenneth Neill Cameron, author of *Shelley and His Circle*, argued that "invasion of privacy more often than not assures fair treatment of famous men." The biographer investigated allegations that Shelley had had an incestuous relationship with his sister and had left his first wife with only fourteen shillings. Both charges proved to be untrue. Indeed, the poet had left Harriet a thousand pounds in the bank and ten thousand more in his will. The biographer J. Donald Adams concluded that the "writing of biography is increasingly difficult for the biographer, but invasion of privacy is necessary."

By 1992 biographers were under more restrictions than had ever been the case in the history of the genre. It became routine for the major review organs to print letters of protest from subjects and their estates. Thus Jonathan Clowes, writing to the *New York Times Book Review* on Doris Lessing's behalf, informed readers that Carole Klein's biography was "totally unauthorized." I like that "totally"—as if biographies could be partially unauthorized. It reminds me of the letter I received from William Abrahams informing me that he was Lillian Hellman's "one and *only* authorized biographer." Did he fear an epidemic? Clowes announced that Klein would be denied permission to quote anything from Lessing's writings, published or unpublished.

Just a few weeks before Clowes's salvo, the F. R. Leavis estate wrote the *TLS* to warn off contributors to an unauthorized life of the controversial critic. And the estate had no intention of authorizing anyone, the letter emphasized. A year later John le Carré, having already deterred Jeffrey Meyers, put a halt to Graham Lord's proposed biography by bringing suit for defamation.

Although the amended copyright act in 1992 made it easier for biographers to do their work, literary figures and their estates continue to invoke the copyright act as a way of restraining recalcitrant biographers.

THE WORD "ADVENTURES" in the subtitle of this book would dismay Richard Ellmann, who wrote in a lecture: "Biography is or should be an act of fellowship, the present reaching out its hand to the past." I don't object to this formulation so much as I gasp at all it leaves out. It makes biography sound so grand, the biographer so noble. Ellmann never wanted to explain—except in the most oblique way—what it had cost him to become a biographer. Writing to Stewart Richardson at J. P. Lippincott, the biographer asked to be excused from submitting the article he had agreed to undertake about the hardships of doing biography. "What struck me at once was how demeaning it was to describe my grubbing around for material. . . . I feel the book [his Joyce biography] speaks for itself. . . ." Surely James Joyce might have said the same to Richard Ellmann, if Joyce had been alive to rebuff—as he surely would have—the biographer's approach. Ellmann's rationale, after all, was the same as Hamilton's: Joyce was an extraordinarily autobiographical writer. Joyce, no less than Salinger, had made a religion of his art. Joyce, almost as much as Salinger, disliked discussing his work, let alone his life. Indeed, how could there even be a J. D. Salinger without a James Joyce? Yet Ellmann became Joyce's St. Paul; Hamilton and the rest of us are Judases.

With the exception of cranky Hugh Kenner, I have never seen a serious attack on Ellmann's Joyce biography, though Brenda Maddox in *Nora* suggested that Ellmann relied too much on Stanislaus. What Ellmann thought of Kenner in private I do not know, but publicly Ellmann never took issue with the critic's charge that the biographer relied too much on the gossip retailed in interviews.

Even critics who dislike biography adore Ellmann. Adore is not too strong a word. Reading the reviews that Ellmann preserved, and that are now in his papers at the University of Tulsa, I have found no detractors. It is no insult to his formidable Joyce biography to say that Ellmann, both inside and outside his book, did everything possible to deflect attention from the darker side of the genre. Other biographers in Ellmann's league—say, George Painter and Leon Edel—have fared nearly as well, but they have certainly not won the kind of affection Ellmann so studiously courted. Boswell remains in first place among students of biography, but he also has had his share of critics. Only Richard Ellmann is *revered*. Only Richard Ellmann is so universally called an artist. And at least part of the reason for his unique standing is his reticence about the hazards and humiliations of biography.

Of course Ellmann is not alone in wanting to cover up the troubled face of biography. In *Tread Softly for You Tread on My Life*, the late Michael King admits to having decided not to publish all he knew about his subjects' sex lives and other intimate matters that "might unjustifiably hurt or offend relatives or associates." What a way to put the matter. Is there a justifiable way of hurting people? If so, virtually any revelation will be available for the biographer to rationalize.

King was one of those ethical biographers as defined by Natasha Spender. He allowed his subject's family to vet his manuscript, calling this censorship his "respect for the living." To King, this kowtowing to family wishes is worth the price of access to sources he would otherwise be denied. Thus King happily excised passages from his biography of Janet Frame that she deemed "too raw or intensely private." King somehow deluded himself into thinking he was not authorized and had retained a degree of independence. After exposing how Frame controlled the biography, he writes (without apparent irony): "I as author have made the final decision about what is and is not to be published . . . she also recognized my right, as a fellow professional, to make final decisions about treatment and content."

The biographer Harry Ricketts observed that King's doctrine of "compassionate truth" amounted to a "retrospective rationalization of the constraints under which King agreed to write his recent life of Janet Frame." In effect, King was "Framed," Ricketts rightfully concludes.

I DOUBT there is any code by which biographers can abide. The nature of the genre depends on the biographer and his subject and on how this tension is handled in the biography itself. I subscribe to a conflict-of-interest theory of biography. There is my interest in writing a book about, say, Susan Sontag. And then there is Susan Sontag's interest in herself. These interests are mutually exclusive. Susan Sontag is the subject of my book, whereas Susan Sontag is the subject of *her* life. Biographers often ignore this fundamental point or won't admit it—at least they won't own up to it when they are writing about writing biographies.

Without this sense of resistance, of friction, I wonder whether biography would be quite so appealing to me. To argue, as Michael King does, that biography is a work of collaboration seems misguided to me. I think the biographer is ultimately his or her own authority. I borrow that phrase from R. G. Collingwood. He has in mind the fact that any genuine work of history is more than the sum of its evidence; it depends, in fact, on the interpreting mind of the historian, who must bring together disparate materials and insights—rather like a detective—into a unified, organic whole. That whole is essentially a story, a narrative of meaning. Otherwise, Collingwood argues, there is only scissors-and-paste history, in which the historian slaps together fragments of evidence and testimony from his sources or authorities. This quilt of fact and speculation might make a rather gaudy design, but it would not be a work of history.

The biographer, I would argue, does much the same thing. Take me, for example. I assemble the following data: a letter from Walter Jackson Bate (at one time the chair of Harvard's English department), a journal kept by Ken Stuart (a student in Lillian Hellman's Harvard writing class), interviews with Hellman's students, interviews with other faculty members who knew Hellman during her Harvard stay, an interview with her physician, and a few newspaper articles. This is the raw material for Chapter 17 of my Hellman biography. If you had all these materials in front of you, they would not add up to Chapter 17. First of all, I don't use all the evidence. Some of it is redundant; some of it is fascinating, and yet there is too much of it to fit into my narrative, which is already burdened with significant detail. I know that readers will stand for only so much material on this phase of Hellman's career. To relate all of it would seriously damage the shape of my book; it would place too much emphasis on this period of Hellman's life.

These kinds of considerations I call aesthetic. I want to write a good book and know I have to be selective. Just as important, however, are the selections I have already made in previous chapters, where I have emphasized Hellman's contentiousness, her pride in her work, her attraction to young people, her generosity, and her tendency to be high-handed. All these qualities I find in my evidence for Chapter 17, though as individual bits of evidence these sources contradict one another. Bate, for example, was offended by an incredibly demanding and insensitive bitch, while Ken Stuart was charmed by her shrewd and patient handling of young writers, including himself. In the writing of the chapter, I hope these seeming contradictions are resolved—that is, that they are understandable given the different contexts Hellman found herself in. With students she would never behave the way she behaved with Bate. He was supposed to be the red-carpet man, the one who should have fawned over her. With Ken Stuart it was just the opposite: Hellman knew she was there to give him something. Nowhere in Chapter 17 do I make this comparison between Hellman's treatment of Bate and Stuart, but I believe it is there in the configuration of my narrative, and that readers who have been following the whole story of my book can find it.

While I was writing my biography of Hellman, I often had a sense of her struggling for possession of my book. There was no doubt in my mind that she did not want me to write it my way. Not just because I would find things out—like her Communist party membership—but because, like a dramatist, I was setting her up in scenes that were not of her own making. I was questioning her memoirs and producing an alternative version of her life.

Speaking only for myself, I hope to tell a good story. Because it is a story, I have to deal with everything, not just my subject's public face. I want the gossip, the intimacies, everything I can find out that made that person what she or he is.

Writing biography is a shameless profession, an exercise in bad taste, and a rude inquiry. Most biographers I have met prefer not to say so in public. We are journalists and sometimes scholars who try very hard to be accurate. But is it any wonder that the biographer's choice gets expressed as the selection of a victim?

A Note on Sources

REBECCA WEST reveled in biography and wrote biographies of St. Augustine and others. But she became deeply troubled about the genre in the 1970s when biographers began to inquire into her fraught relationships with her lover H. G. Wells and their son, Anthony West. A kind of biographical war ensued between mother and son, resulting in Gordon Ray's *H. G. Wells and Rebecca West* (1974), which West sanctioned, and Anthony West's *H. G. Wells: Aspects of a Life* (1984). Rebecca West's reservations about contemporary biography did not deter her, however, from contributing her reminiscences about her fellow literary figures to scores of biographies by others. Like many critics of biography, she helped industrious biographers to flourish—including her own, designating two biographers to write the long and the short versions of her life. She also published an important, if overlooked, essay on the role of biography in literary criticism: "Tradition in Criticism," an attack on T. S. Eliot's theory of impersonality in "Tradition and the Individual Talent." West's essay appeared in *Tradition and Experiment in Present-Day Literature* (1929).

Joyce Carol Oates employed her influential term "pathography" in a review of David Roberts's *Jean Stafford* (*New York Times*, August 28, 1988). Bitter *Fame*, Anne Stevenson's biography of Sylvia Plath, appeared in 1989. Michiko Kakutani's *New York Times* article about bloodsport biography was published on May 20, 1994.

The comment on literary biography as part of "cutting-edge commercialism" appears in the *Irish Times*, September 17, 1994.

Helen Dudar's review of my "dishy" biography appeared on the front page of the *New York Times Book Review* (May 8, 1988).

My revised biography of Martha Gellhorn was published in 2003 and the first edition in 1990. For Hywell Williams's view of biography as a peepshow, see the *Guardian*, June 7, 2002.

Robert McCrum's article on biography is in the June 25, 2000, issue of the *Observer*.

Janet Malcolm published her book on Plath and her biographers in 1994 and *The Journalist and the Murderer* in 1990.

Steven Millhauser's *Edwin Mullhouse* was published in 1972, and Jean-Paul Sartre's *Nausea* in 1938.

2

James Atlas invoked Martin Amis's take on biography in *Brill's Content*, Fall 2001. Iain Finlayson published his biography of Robert Browning in 2004. William Golding's update of Browning's view of biography appears in *The Paper Men* (1984), which seems to be a favorite of biographers I have interviewed.

Flaubert's Parrot, Julian Barnes's meditation on biography, was published in 1985.

Margaret Drabble's "Digging in the Wild Garden" is available at www.kingston.ac.uk/cusp/Lectures/Drabblelhtm.

I discuss the 1963 Edinburgh Festival in *The Lives of Norman Mailer* (1991) and in *Rebecca West: A Saga of the Century* (1995).

Fiona McCarthy wrote about her Eric Gill biography in "Baptism of Fire," *Guardian*, July 24, 2004.

I will deal with my work on the Jill Craigie biography in a forthcoming book, *Adventures of an Outlaw: A Biographer at Work*.

3

Michael Ratcliffe's *Observer* piece was published December 29, 2001, A. S. Byatt's review in the *Guardian*, February 21, 2004, and

John Sutherland's "Age of Blackwash" in the *Guardian*, October 29, 2001.

The "art is sacred" comment can be found in the Readerville.com forum biography discussion group. Sherman Alexie made his comment in a *Salon* thread on writers' lives.

For Philip Hensher on Peter Conradi's Iris Murdoch biography, see the *Spectator*, September 15, 2001.

For biography as a butcher's business, see the *Independent*, September 17, 1994, and the *New Statesman and Nation*, September 2, 1994, for the comment equating biography with pornography.

Paul John Eakin's *The Ethics of Life Writing* was published in 2004. Joseph J. Ellis's take on "homicidal biography" can be found in the *New York Times*, May 18, 2000, and Nicholas Shakespeare's comment on biography as murder in the *Daily Telegraph*, April 15, 2000.

Nabokov published *The Real Life of Sebastian Knight* in 1941. On the biographer's hostility toward his subject, see Jeffrey Meyers, "Johnson, Boswell, and Modern Biography," *New Criterion*, November 2002.

Martha Gellhorn's attempt to use the Author's Guild as a weapon against me came as a surprise when a Guild attorney told me about it at a New York University biography seminar meeting. Georgina Howell's summary of my book appeared in the *Sunday Times Magazine*, April 8, 2001.

4

Jenny Uglow's biography of Elizabeth Gaskell, *A Habit of Stories*, was published in 1993.

Scott E. Caspar, in *Constructing American Lives* (1999), is one of the few scholars to examine carefully the beginnings of biography in America.

Annette Gordon-Reed published her study of Thomas Jefferson and Sally Hemings in 1997. It is telling that Fawn Brodie, the only historian to take the liaison seriously, was also a woman.

Lucasta Miller's *The Brontë Myth* (2001) is essential reading for any student of biography.

William Phillips published *A Partisan View* in 1999.

Jeffrey Meyers's *The Spirit of Biography* (1989) is refreshing for its candor and insight.

Joan Givner published her memoir, *The Self-Portrait of a Biographer*, in 1993.

5

Somerset Maugham first published *Cakes and Ale* in 1930. Michael Foot's two-volume *Aneurin Bevan: A Biography* (1962, 1974) is one of the classic political biographies of the twentieth century.

6

My polemic "Biography High and Low or God Bless Kitty Kelley!" appeared in *Biography*, Spring 1997. George Carpozi, Jr., published *Poison Pen: The Unauthorized Biography of Kitty Kelley* in 1991.

Montaigne's comments on biography appear in his essay "Of Books."

Jerry Oppenheimer's *Martha Stewart: Just Desserts: The Unauthorized Biography* appeared in 1997.

I published *Biography: An Annotated Bibliography* in 1992 and updated this work in "Biography as a Genre," *Choice*, October 1997.

7

Samuel Johnson's definitive essay on biography appears in *The Rambler*, No. 60, frequently included in anthologies of his writing.

Gellhorn's authorized biographer is Caroline Moorehead, and my review of her book appeared in the *New York Sun*, October 8, 2003.

In *The Hitler of History* (1997), John Lukacs has produced an extraordinary work of historiography that is essential to an understanding of biography—as is Herbert Butterfield's classic *George III and the Historians* (1958).

Richard Holmes published *Dr. Johnson and Mr. Savage* in 1993. His autobiographical *Footsteps* (1985) and *Sidetracks* (2000), his essays about biography, belong on the shelf of any serious student of biography.

8

Adam Sisman's *Boswell's Presumptuous Task* (2000) has rightly been hailed as a thrilling reenactment of the stages by which his subject created the greatest of English biographies.

9

In *Anthony Burgess: A Biography* (2002), Roger Lewis not only presents a candid view of Ellmann, he transforms the genre of biography into a form of energetic and amusing criticism that has shocked most reviewers. Burgess emerges as a fascinating phony worth study because he was so adept at performing the charade of a great author. I find Lewis's savaging of biographical conventions rousing and refreshing. See my review in the *New York Sun*, March 3, 2004.

10

All the Ellmann correspondence may be found in the special collections department of McFarlin Library at the University of Tulsa. There you will find that Ellmann relied on his wife Mary (herself a formidable literary critic) to hold his family together while he journeyed around Europe in quest of Joycean material. Her letters to him are sometimes testy and even resentful, especially on those days when she would have to organize his voluminous mail and then report to him via aerograms about all the business entailed in researching a biography.

11

The details in this chapter about Boswell's behavior as a biographer are culled from Adam Sisman's engaging *Boswell's Presumptuous Task* (2000).

Paul Theroux published *Sir Vidia's Shadow: A Friendship Across Five Continents* in 1998.

Peter Ackroyd's *Dickens* appeared in 1990, and Donald Spoto's *Marilyn Monroe* in 1993.

Bernard Crick published *George Orwell: A Life* in 1980; Michael Shelden published *George Orwell: The Authorised Biographer* in 1991. I admire Shelden, whose principles seem to remain the same whether or not he is authorized. See, for example, his brilliant *Graham Greene: The Enemy Within* (1995). Shelden, as well as Jeffrey Meyers in *George Orwell: Wintry Conscience of a Generation* (2000), are candid biographers beset by those who would favor a more genteel approach to the genre. Their work provoked Hilary Spurling's whitewash of Sonia Orwell: *The Girl from the Fiction Department* (2003). For a critique of Spurling and the Orwell biographers, see Doug Munro, "Silences and Evasions: The Biographer Spurling and the Widow Orwell," in *Biography and Source Studies* 8 (2004).

Lawrance Thompson published his three-volume biography of Frost between 1966 and 1976 (the last volume completed by R. H. Winnick). Subsequently other biographers, especially Jeffrey Meyers in *Robert Frost* (1996), have built upon Thompson's much criticized work.

Adam Sisman takes issue with Macaulay's view that Boswell was a fool, and because he was a fool was able to write a candid biography that vividly portrayed his subject. A more sophisticated man, a more dignified man, would not have abased himself before Johnson in this manner, Macaulay argues. But how could a fool write a literary masterpiece?—especially one that was so carefully planned and executed—a fact Macaulay could not appreciate since Boswell's papers were not discovered or studied until the twentieth century, Sisman points out. But it seems to me that Macaulay was essentially right. Boswell was a fool and a genius. I don't believe that literary talent and foolishness are mutually exclusive.

Hilary Mills published *Mailer: A Biography* in 1982.

Aurum Press (London) will publish *To Be a Woman: The Life of Jill Craigie* in the spring of 2005. My essay on doing the Craigie biography will appear in the forthcoming *Adventures of an Outlaw: A Biographer at Work*.

12

A. O. J. Cockshut's *Truth to Life: The Art of Biography in the Nineteenth Century* (1974) is rather iconoclastic in its assertion that the genre experienced a "golden age." And while I am skeptical about his claim, he has done more than most critics to show that there is a biographical aesthetic quite as sophisticated and profound as that of the novel.

Shelley's view of poets as legislators is expressed in his essay "Defense of Poetry."

My assessment of Carlyle relies heavily on Cockshut's penetrating analysis.

13

See Cockshut's *Truth to Life* for perceptive discussions of Trevelyan and Morley as biographers.

Ian Hamilton, *Keepers of the Flame* (1994), and Cockshut have stimulating discussions of Froude. I rely on these two authors as well as on James Anthony Froude's remarkable *My Relations with Carlyle* (written in 1886, published in 1903). Phyllis Rose's *Parallel Lives* (1983) has an insightful chapter about the Carlyles.

14

Was Aldington deliberately echoing Carlyle's disdain for mealy-mouthed biographers? I do not know. After much delay—caused mainly by Aldington's opponents—his biography of T. E. Lawrence appeared in 1955.

I am deeply indebted to Fred Crawford's illuminating *Richard Aldington and Lawrence of Arabia: A Cautionary Tale* (1998).

Leo Braudy published *The Frenzy of Renown: Fame and Its History* in 1997.

Michael Millgate's *Testamentary Acts* (1992) is more scholarly than Ian Hamilton's *Keepers of the Flame*, and though their studies overlap somewhat, they should be read together to see how difficult it is for biographers to gain access to the full records of their subjects' lives.

The Quest for Corvo: An Experiment in Biography by A. J. A. Symons appeared in 1934, Ian Hamilton's *In Search of J. D. Salinger* in 1988, and *Nothing Ever Happens to the Brave: The Story of Martha Gellhorn* in 1990.

Paul Johnson's singularly apposite review of Aldington's T. E. Lawrence biography appeared in *New Statesman and Nation*, May 5, 1956.

Eudora: A Writer's Life appeared in 1998, *Doris Lessing: A Biography* by Carole Klein in 2000, *The Unruly Life of Woody Allen* by Marion Meade in 2000, and *Telling Women's Lives: The New Biography* in 1994.

Craig Seligman's fatuous *Sontag & Kael* was published in 2004.

15

For Leon Edel on modern biographers and archives, see *Writing Lives: Principia Biographia* (1984).

One instance of a subject helping her unauthorized biographer is Gloria Steinem. She had a change of heart in regard to Sydney Ladensohn's *Gloria Steinem: Her Passions, Politics, and Mystique* (1997). Steinem was disappointed in the work of her authorized biographer, Carolyn Heilbrun, even though *The Education of a Woman: The Life of Gloria Steinem* (1996) seemed to most critics to verge on hagiography. Stern, a friend of mine, admits that as soon as Steinem began cooperating with her, the biographer began to soften her criticism. It can be seductive to deal with a powerful subject like Steinem—or simply awkward not to adopt her view of certain matters, not to mention the gratitude a biographer feels for the subject's cooperation. Nevertheless Steinem was no more satisfied with Stern's biography than she was with Heilbrun's, and Stern had to endure the spectacle of Steinem hunting down the biographer's interviewees and pressuring them to recant some of their testimony. For subjects like Gloria Steinem it is doubtful that any biographer could ultimately prove acceptable.

16

Louise DiSalvo published her biography of Virginia Woolf in 1990. She told me that work with Beacon Press on establishing some modicum of fair use entailed her hiring her own attorney.

Natasha Spender's proposal for policing biographers appears in the October 9, 1992, issue of the *Times Literary Supplement,* and John Lahr's article on biography in the *Evening Standard,* September 26, 1992.

Ann Thwaite's biography of A. A. Milne appeared in 1990.

Hugh David published his unauthorized *Stephen Spender: A Portrait with Background* in 1992.

17

Brenda Maddox's *Nora* appeared in 1988.

Michael King's collected essays about his biographies, *Tread Softly for You Tread on My Life,* were published in 2001. Harry Ricketts's review of King's book appeared in *New Zealand Books,* March 2002.

18

R. G. Collingwood's *Idea of History* was first published in 1946. I first read it as an undergraduate in 1966, and I do not believe there is another book of its kind that has influenced my work as a biographer more deeply.

Index

A NOTE ON THE AUTHOR

Carl Rollyson has written biographies of Rebecca West, Norman Mailer, Martha Gellhorn, Lillian Hellman, Marilyn Monroe, and (with Lisa Paddock) Susan Sontag. Mr. Rollyson has also written or edited a number of literary studies and reference works, among them *Reading Susan Sontag*, *Herman Melville A to Z*, and *Critical Survey of Long Fiction*. He is professor of English at Baruch College of the City University of New York, and lives in Cape May County, New Jersey.